The Coming Storm

Steve Ashley

To all the young people that are trying to make their way in their lives. May you prosper and be happy.

Table of Contents

Section 1 – Failing Institutions

There is a storm coming. A storm the like maybe we have never seen before in the history of our country. It will have many parallels with things that have happened in the past. But it will be different in many ways and maybe much more devastating. The average citizen of the United States is very close to losing their basic freedoms. I know that's a big, big statement. But let's look at some of the facts that really can't be disputed.

We have, for many years, been completely sold-out by the political class in our country. Right and left, federal, state and local, the blame belongs to everyone. They have and are designing a system and a set of rules that you must play by, a system that impoverishes you and keeps you docile so they can rule and dictate how you must live. The greatest threat to the average citizen is not citizens of a different color or belief. It's the political class and the elite media that are not smart or gifted in any way. Over the last seventy years, they have almost completely sold-out the country. In almost all cases, they have made the monetary calculation, whether it benefits them to be on the right or the left of politics only for the purpose of enriching themselves. For you to have any chance of weathering the storm to come and keep your freedom and even your dignity, you need to look at some of the unpleasant truths and start to make plans now. You cannot depend on any political party to protect you. They're incapable of that. Only you, as an individual, have the power to save yourself.

Before we go any farther, this is not a political book in the sense I am trying to sell you on a political party or belief system; I generally despise both parties. They are both run by mostly very ignorant people that are primarily opportunists that hope and pray they'll be gone with their pensions and book deals and loot before they have to answer for their failures.

You might classify me as a conservative but not in the political sense but conservative in my life and how I approach problems in everyday life. In the chapters to follow, we'll talk about some of the ways we got to this sorry state we're in and some of the ways you might be able to protect yourself when the storm hits. Make no mistake. The storm is coming, but no one knows the date it will make landfall. Being optimistic is always a good trait but looking at reality is much more important. This is not a time to just wish things were different.

The first way to empower yourself is to try to be well-informed on the true state of the nation.

There are many so-called leaders and people of so-called goodwill that will lie to you every day to get you to conform to what they, in their wisdom, think is best for you or some way they can profit off their actions. All people that are trying to sell you something, be it a product or an idea, in the end, have a strong motivation to try to make you obey. There has never been a more important time to think for yourself and take actions that, in the end, may benefit you or your loved ones.

If you think for a moment, imagine the country as a corporation or wealthy family that at one time had a lot of assets. And over the years and through changes in management or generations of family members, made bad decisions on top of bad decisions until there was virtually no assets left to draw on, only more borrowed money. You start to see where we are as a nation. With corporations or wealthy families or nations as the end game gets closer, the decisions and the borrowing become more frantic, and the people that have been the leaders and decision-makers start to look for excuses that will exonerate them from their sins.

In 2020 the perfect excuse has arrived in the form of Covid-19. You will start to hear all our decisions were smart and sound. We were 'done in' by an outside event that was outside of our control, but the real truth is the die was cast a long time before that. Let's start to talk about some of the institutions that have completely failed us over the last seventy or seventy-five years, from the end of World War II, when we were the strongest country in the history of the world, to a country that appears strong but is really quite weak compared to those days. Our first example of a failed enterprise is our news agencies that have become part of our political parties and part Hollywood entertainment, but in most cases, are not honest brokers of the news.

In the first section of this book, I talk about many of the ways we have gotten into the sorry state we're in. In the second section, I'll lay out a lot of concrete steps you, as an individual or a family, can take to help you weather the storm to come. Steps that anyone can take no matter your income to make you stronger in your life without buying or investing in anything only changing the way you live now to build a more prosperous, safe and happy future. In section three, which is a bonus section entitled 'Into the Country,' I will lay out some of the pitfalls and advantages of buying rural property. If you're dreaming of moving from a large city to a more secure place, this will be of value to you.

Chapter 1 – So Much Time, So Little Information

In the old days that really weren't that long ago, the three major networks had an hour news show in the early evening. Then there were their Sunday morning shows, usually with the same wise men and women every week. This was pretty much the network's contribution to the news business each week. That and a subscription to a national or big-city newspaper and your local paper might keep you reasonably informed. In those days, the newspapers were still making money and, in most cases, could afford to hire some very good investigative reporters to do in-depth feature stories. Now with only a very few exceptions, all the papers are running on empty with a lot less staff, and the local papers are a disaster. A few abbreviated stories cut and pasted from the wire services, a few lost dog stories, and it takes about five minutes to read. They have even fewer staff, and their goal is to get something out each day and hope you don't notice that there is really nothing there except comics, obituaries and puzzles.

We are now in the land of 24-7 cable news. Think about that, twenty-four hours a day, every day - the luxury of time to report in-depth on anything of interest to the general public. They also can put almost any person from whatever field on the air for really as long as they want, and all you get is three-minute fluff pieces all day long. You have an expert newsreader with an earpiece and an invisible producer talking in their ear. The guests or paid contributors that had gotten all dressed up to come to the station and be on the show get their three to five minutes to try to make their point with most times a lot of interruptions. Then the invisible producer determines that most people are bored, and we go to a fluff piece about an escaped elephant on the freeway.

Let's take the example of two stories – one large and one small. The Trump/Russia investigation, no matter which side of the political aisle you're on, is a hell of a story, the kind of story that makes a great novel or wins Pulitzer prizes. If some investigative reporter that has worked diligently on the story comes on FOX news, for example, he or she may get a few minutes to talk about their research. On the other cable networks, there seems to be a complete blackout on the story. A reasonable person of either political party might have a lot of questions, but they never get answered.

The second example is a smaller story but important to the person being highlighted in the story. A woman in Huston, Texas, is about to be evicted from her apartment, where she has lived fourteen years. According to the story, she lost her job because of Covid-19 and is drawing unemployment. It is not stated in the article how much her state unemployment is, but we know she is getting that and six hundred dollars extra from the Federal government plus a check for twelve hundred dollars from the stimulus bill. How did she get into financial trouble so fast? Is she working with her landlord and is the landlord working with her? Did she have a good payment record before she was laid off? It's reasonable to assume that up to eight or nine hundred dollars a week, she should have been made whole by the extra stimulus check and extra unemployment, but we will never know. The story is big on emotion and very small on facts - laziness on the part of the reporter and the network.

There are hundreds of stories a week that run purely on emotions but no facts. One of the most important institutions in the country is a free-press with all the time and resources in the world to keep people informed and is, in most cases, a complete failure. They want to run their commercials and sell their books and be thought of as smart people, but in the end, they are failing their basic mandate. Most of the newsreaders are very poor interviewers. There are some obvious exceptions, but for the most part, they interrupt constantly. Most of them and the producers believe the average viewer only has an attention span of a couple of minutes at most.

Unfortunately, in some cases, they may be right. There are large groups of people in the country that, for whatever reason, are almost completely uninformed. They don't know the names of their senators or state representatives or anything about the pressing questions of the day or the history of the country. The only time these people become important to the news media is a couple of months before an election when the talking heads can more or less tell them how to vote. The next time you watch a news show, after a couple of stories, write down the obvious questions to which you would like to have answers. I call it the six basic questions test. In almost all cases, it will fail miserably. We have never had more news sources in the country and so little news or information of any value.

We still have a lot of smart people in the country that have valuable things to say, but they are being marginalized and censored by the news agencies and some social media platforms daily. All this also applies to the business news channels that, for the most part, are shills for only one thing - the stock market. The only game they really want you to play. Much more about the stock market later on.

Chapter 2 – The Federal Reserve

One of the least understood agencies in the government is the Federal Reserve, and they like it that way. They can go about their work without a lot of scrutiny from the average citizen. Unfortunately, they are not understood by our elective representatives either. For years you could watch Senate and House hearings with Alan Greenspan holding forth on some topic that no one in the hearing room understood and, in most cases, didn't have any meaning anyway. Then each member of the committee would read a question or two that had been generated by their staff to make them look smart or well-informed. In the end, it came down to do anything you want Mr. Greenspan, but we don't want any downturn in the economy, no corrections of any kind, only forward progress.

You would never get through a speech from any member of the Fed without the speaker saying that we're really worried about the savings rate of the people in the country. People just aren't saving what they should. And then in their ultimate wisdom, they destroyed traditional savings for the average person – maybe forever. The time of almost zero interest rates had arrived. We could fill many pages with the events and times of that happening, but all we need to know is that it happened. That single decision has all but destroyed the savings and interest rate model that has served us well for most of the country's history. This decision had destroyed the retirement plans of many small savers that depended upon interest from bank CDs and were at an age in their lives when the last thing they needed was to start chasing yields in the stock markets or low-grade bonds. This is a perfect example of the power of government to only give you one game to play - the game that benefits their friends on Wall Street. The willful blindness of the Fed is truly remarkable.

In about 2006, TV shows about house-flipping became all the rage. One of the first ones I saw featured a brother and sister in California who bought a house of approximately 1200 square feet in need of a lot of renovation for $680,000. Then with the idea of spending about $80,000 on repairs, try for a retail price of $910,000. At the time, it could have been built with the land and all new construction in the Mid-West for less than $150,000. My first question was, what bank in their right mind would give a $680,000 loan on a house like that and what bank would loan $910,000 on the same place a few months later.

These shows went on until the crash of 2008. If I had been a member of the Fed, I would have wanted to know more right away, but it seemed just not to raise any red flags with the super-smart people. Just before the crash, one agency in my town had about eight closings a day on houses that could probably never be paid for with people that had lied about their incomes with the help in some cases of the mortgage company. Every closing was generating about $3,000 in fees, with people getting rich shuffling paper, and in the end, no one went to jail or paid any price at all. Even a lot of the people that bought houses weren't hit that bad. They had no real money invested and, in some cases, got to live free in their home for years before the banks could get to them to foreclose.

One of the bedrock ways for the average person to build wealth is to buy a house they can afford, try to pay it off at some point, and regular savings that might yield four to six percent safely over the long haul. By their actions, the Fed upended the housing market by not taking action early on when the bubble was forming, and their zero-interest policy disrupted one of the most important pillars of wealth creation in the country. There are bailouts for all the bad actors but none for the little guy that always gets stuck with the bill in the end. Thanks so much for your leadership, Alan, and all the rest of you economic geniuses.

Chapter 3 – Closest to the People

One of the constant sayings of the right is 'the government that is closest to the people works the best,' but in reality, it hasn't worked out that way. I'll use my old hometown as a model for what has happened to towns and cities all over America from the end of World War II until the present. Rockford, Illinois, was a city of about 90,000 people at the end of World War II and about 145,000 today, which is down about eight percent from its all-time high. We were known as the machine tool capital of the world up through maybe 1975. We had a tremendous industrial base. We not only made almost every metal part you could think of, but we also made the machines that made the parts. For about twenty-five years after the war, most of the factories worked ten hours a day, five days a week, and maybe five hours or more on Saturdays - a lot of overtime for a lot of workers. We were a factory town that didn't look like a factory town. Most of the factories were consigned to one area of the city, and we had many beautiful residential neighborhoods with more being built. All the workers with steady jobs and overtime pay could afford to buy new homes of

1200 to 1400 square feet, which in a lot of cases were called 'Rockford Ranches.' It was a relatively easy time to start to enter the middle-class with the prospect that you could stay there. People came from all over the country to work in Rockford. We had a good bus system that took care of our public transportation, and most school children could walk to neighborhood schools with no need for a large school bus system. Two other large assets were our police department that had always been virtually scandal-free, and a conservative local newspaper. The city had a lot going for it.

Then sometime in the seventies, it started to change. It was decided to take part of our prosperous downtown and close up some of the main streets and make it a pedestrian mall. There was resistance from many business owners, but the powers to be, with a great deal of help from our newspaper, prevailed. In short order after that, it was decided to build a Metro Center to bring entertainment to our citizens. In was voted down several times but in the end, the powers-to-be prevailed. The city was starting to get into the entertainment business. One day the newspaper had an editorial that stated, "A city rises and falls on the quality of entertainment it can provide its people." I have always thought that was one of the most insane statements I had ever seen in print. But we were only getting started on our long descent. We were beginning to enter a time of city leaders building monuments to themselves with taxpayer money that should have gone to basic infrastructure and supporting our industrial base.

Then sometime in the early eighties, it became fashionable with the elite thinkers, both nationally and locally, to start thinking that we didn't need any heavy manufacturing in our country anymore. Send all those dirty factories to some other part of the world. Our people will all become computer programmers or work in some kind of service industry. It all sounded so wonderful. We'll retrain everyone for the new economy.

The next event in our city may have had the most lasting and devastating effect on our long term health. The city was suddenly in Federal Court charged with racism in our school system, and the city was under court order with a Federal judge empowered to spend city money as he saw fit for years. At the end of the day, after about two billion dollars, we had a lot of new bricks-and-mortar in new school buildings but no real improvement in education. That's when real estate taxes really got out of hand, and people started to vote with their feet and got out of town fast. There again, the local newspaper was the biggest cheerleader for the new taxes that were killing the city all for really no gain in the end.

I would like to report on some decision that the leaders of the city have made in the last seventy years that has had lasting value for the city, but I can't really think of any other than a few very small successes. Our industrial base is mostly gone. We have some of the highest real-estate taxes in the country. Our poverty rate is through the roof, and we have a crime rate that, on a per capita basis, is probably as bad as Chicago. Like everyone else, we are paying for three workforces of city employees – two that are retired and one on the job. Twenty-five or thirty percent of the city budget goes to pensions before they spend a dime on anything else. With our high real-estate taxes and an eight and a quarter percent sales tax, we are counting heavily on casino gambling and marijuana sales to stay afloat. The entry-level for our young people trying to get a foothold on the middle-class is getting dimmer by the day.

And the all-powerful local newspaper is down most days to four or five pages of obituaries, comics and puzzles with little news. They brought almost all of it on themselves. They never thought about their customers, the taxpayers. They never saw a taxing scheme they didn't love.

Chapter 4 – State Government

I have lived my whole life in the state of Illinois. Like my old hometown, I have watched the slow descent into bankruptcy. First off, Illinois has been the home of a lot of bad actors over a lot of years. We have a time-honored tradition of sending our governors to jail, along with a lot of minor players that have made off with millions and millions of taxpayer funds over the years. The amazing thing is no one seems to get too mad about the state of the Land of Lincoln.

A lot of states are having a hard time paying their bills, mostly self-imposed. But Illinois is almost in a class by itself. We are so past the point of no return that it is nearly ludicrous to think about stabilizing the situation. Without a federal bailout that is being discussed in Washington as I write this, Illinois will go broke very soon. It will, of course, be blamed on Covid-19 but that will only be the last nail in the coffin.

If you think about the awesome power of a state government, almost everything that moves in a state is taxed. The state is a silent partner in every business. Our latest governor, a man short on talent and vision that is very rich with inherited wealth, has managed in a short time to have doubled the gas tax and fees on anything he could think of and is working hard on a graduated income tax and expanding marijuana sales and gambling as much as possible. But the real truth is all of that will only help at the margins. The die is already cast. No super good economy or period of prosperity will fill up the state coffers.

The masthead of Illinois government ought to be 'Public employee unions eat first. After they are finished at the table, any scraps left may be divided up for the little people.' Let's look at a true example of the generosity of the state for chosen people that will always vote for the people in power. A state highway worker that is fifty-eight years old that retires would normally get seventy percent of final pay. But because he worked on the highway, that is deemed 'hazardous,' so his pension is eighty-five percent of final salary. The final salary was $68,500; eighty-five percent is $58,225 plus a three percent cost of living bonus into perpetuity - a generous bonus by anyone's standards. But we're not done. Before the fifty-eight year old retired, he married a thirty-eight-year-old woman and got her vested on his pension. So if she lives to ninety, the state will have paid him or her a total of fifty-two years with the pension going up three percent a year. After less than six years, he is at full pay before retirement. At the end of 52 years, the state would have paid out $7,356,559. No government can afford this, and that's only for one employee. There are no private pensions that payout like this. It's impossible in the long run. If you figured money in a CD in a bank at one point five percent interest that you might get if you're lucky in today's environment, you would need about four million dollars to pay this one pension.

But the money isn't there. It's all on future taxpayers of our children trying to make a decent life for themselves. In the meantime, taxpayers that are trying to save for their retirement are living in a time of almost no returns on their savings. No one wants to deny these people a pension, but it has to be fair. And don't fall for the line that it's the state's fault for not putting enough money away each year. It was never there to put away ever. If you look at the fiscal health of Illinois versus say Wisconsin, it's a breathtaking difference. You might want to vote with your feet.

Most taxpayers didn't promise a lavish pension to anyone. Public pensions are the greatest generational theft in the history of our country on all levels of government. We made what amounts to an illegal deal. We'll give you whatever you want. Just keep voting for us.

I know this is another uplifting chapter, but I believe it's an honest assessment of a lot of states and cities. You might want to look at the interesting health of Chicago finances also – a city that's mostly run by the teachers union with their four months a year off.

Chapter 5 – The Car Companies

Another game you will, at some point, be made to play is the electric car game. This will be a classic government game where they make the rules of the game, and you must obey. All the car companies in the world have gone all-in on electric cars to the tune of about 225 billion dollars. This is maybe the largest industrial roll of the dice in history going all-in on a concept that doesn't have a large customer base already established.

At some point, the companies will be in financial distress again, like 2008, when the Obama administration bailed out GM and Chrysler. The next bailout will probably consist of an additional two or three dollar a gallon tax on gasoline to make electric cars somewhat equal to gas-powered vehicles.

To the average person, buying a $40,000 electric car is tantamount to committing economic suicide. No one, for a long time, will know the residual value of a three to a five-year-old electric vehicle or how long the battery pack will last or how efficient they will be in cold climates. It will be millions of miles to know any of these things. Would you rather spend $20,000 to $25,000 on a gas-powered car and spend the other $15,000 to $20,000 on gas as needed or spend $40,000 upfront for something you don't know how it will perform over a number of years. If you think of the extra financing costs, sales tax and insurance, it's not even a close call to go with the gas-powered car.

But none of this will make any difference when the government decides it's time for you to buy electric. If you try to keep your old car or fairly new gas-powered vehicle, you will probably pay a new gas-powered car tax or a global warming tax of some kind. When the government bailout of the car companies comes again, it will be the same old story. We can't do without these basic industries, just like it was said in 2008.

This is all speculation on my part, but I think it will come to pass. The corporations have all the political clout – you don't. You only have to look at Tesla's stock price to know the elites at some point will be bailed out again. The stock price of Tesla is a bubble that has formed before our eyes and seems to get bigger each day.

Chapter 6 – Bricks and Mortar Commercial Real Estate

Another thing to watch closely is the possible death of retail stores in the country. We are already pretty far down the road to a lot less main street retailing. Over the last twenty years, this industry has been greatly overbuilt.

One of the most startling overbuilding was started a few years ago with building bank branches on every corner. I might be the exception, but with direct-deposit, I haven't been physically in a bank for over five years. Now you see a lot of them boarded up and for sale. I don't know what bankers made this decision to have electronic banking and still build a lot of bricks and mortar buildings.

Most people have now become very comfortable with online shopping, and the malls of the world are, in most cases, not destination places anymore, and many of them are showing their age. A lot of cities will, in the future, be looking at a lower real estate tax base and a lot of empty stores. An empty big box store is, in most cases is a real boat anchor and not much good for anything else. A lot of bank loans secured by commercial real estate will start to look not so secure in the future, and a lot of retail jobs will be lost.

This is another area rife for some kind of government bailout. The trend in retail shopping could be greatly exacerbated by Covid-19 or looting or shop-lifting with no penalties. Almost every day in the Wall Street Journal, there is another household name in retailing filing for Chapter 11 bankruptcy. Great numbers of people shopping and working from home have to make a lot of real estate worth less.

Only time will tell who will be the winners and losers, but it has the potential to change a lot of carefully laid plans of a lot of investors and real estate trusts

Chapter 7 – Attorney-General Bill Barr

I have great respect for Attorney-General Barr. I have watched his career from the first time he was attorney-general. He has a well-deserved reputation of a fair man and a top legal mind. I think he may have been the best pick of the Trump administration. The right man at the right time, and I can't find anything he has done in his second time in the job that hasn't been honorable and forthright.

A few days ago, he appeared voluntarily before the house judiciary committee chaired by Jerrold Nadler of New York. It was the worst display of out-and-out thuggery I have ever seen in the House of Representatives in my whole life. I have seen a lot of very unsavory people hauled up before the house judiciary committee over a lot of years to answer for their indiscretions, and I have never seen anyone treated the way Mr. Barr was treated. He was viciously attacked by every democratic member, accused of every crime in the book, not allowed to answer any questions, and even denied a five-minute break at one point by Chairman Nadler. I have never heard or seen anyone denied a break in any committee of Congress. If this is the treatment of a fine, respected man that, at one point, was lauded by the right and the left, we are getting close to ungovernable.

Without civility and common respect, we can't go forward as a country. All the Democrats on the committee ought to be deeply, deeply embarrassed, but we're way past that now.

Chapter 8 – Tucker Carlson

In chapter one, I hit the news agencies real hard. They deserve it and more. Now I'll call out one of the really good people in the news business. I think Tucker Carlson is the most interesting personality in the news business today. First off, he is not afraid. That in itself is marvelous. He is an equal opportunity basher of the left or right side of politics. He asks the obvious questions and the tough questions. Think of the freedom that gives a journalist actually to report what is happening in the country. It also makes you a hated person. The left tries to destroy him on a daily basis. They go after his sponsors, and they have gone to his home and tried to terrify his family besides the ever-present 'he's a racist' label. If we had a half-dozen like him in every newsroom in the country, the news business might start to recover some of what it has lost.

People that report the news should not be friends with the political parties. They should be brave enough to bash bad ideas and bad behavior on both sides of the aisle. The funny thing is he has a very highly rated show. You would think some of the other networks would at least pay attention to that. He resonates with a lot of people that want to see the system held to account. Both Tucker and President Trump have a knack for asking the questions the elites don't want to be answered, and they both pay a very dear price for it. Please keep up the good work, Tucker.

Chapter 9 – Trump as a Democrat

When it looked like General Eisenhower might run for President back in the 1950s, no one knew if he was a democrat or republican. Both parties courted him. The only time in my life that has happened and both parties would have gladly embraced him. In 2015 no one really knew if Donald Trump was a democrat or republican. There were indications but no hard facts.

For the sake of our little story, let's say that Trump had declared he was running as a Democrat, challenged Hilary Clinton for the nomination, and won, and Jeb Bush had won the Republican nomination. It would have been a dream scenario for the left. If Trump - wins, fine. If he loses, Jeb will govern more or less as a democrat anyway. The Bush's always do, and it would have made the George Will, Peggy Noonan wing of the Republican Party very happy. President Obama would have come out with a statement of support for Trump even if he had to hold his nose.

If Trump had won, there would not have been any Russian investigation or phony impeachment or talk of a modern Hitler, just talk on the left of our wonderful new President. Any party that was starting to embrace Michael Avenatty as a possible presidential candidate would have had no problem with Trump. Without looking into the man Tucker Carlson calls 'The Creepy Porn Lawyer.' CNN was about to give him their whole network in primetime every night to bash Trump and get his potential campaign off the ground.

While Rome burns and the country gets closer to bankruptcy, these people collect their pay and play their games with no regard for the future.

Chapter 10 – On the Road

During the depression of the 1930s, we witnessed a mass migration in the country. People were fleeing from the dust bowl to make their way to the Promised Land of California. I wrote a book a few years ago on the depression. It's a sad chapter in our history. You could spend a couple of hours watching the movie 'The Grapes of Wrath' and get a sense of the migration.

We are starting to see people fleeing from what amounts to economic servitude in a lot of states and cities that are mostly run by liberals where forward economic progress has almost become impossible for the average citizen keeping in mind that no one is really average. It is still too early to know what this migration will look like in the end. Will Texas at some point turn into California? Will the old rust belt states of the Midwest see a change in their fortunes?

People are starting to understand that both the East and West coasts of our country have turned into the old company store model. We give you what appears to be high wages and salaries and then take it all back in housing costs, taxes and fees. Add that to the very real prospect of ever-rising crime rates and social unrest and failing schools, and it's no wonder that people are fleeing. Actually, they're running for their fiscal and economic lives.

It will be fascinating to see how this new migration unfolds. One central question will be will these fleeing herds bring their old politics with them to the new places like plague carriers? In a few years, will the new place look like the old? Technology is going to accelerate this migration more every day. The pandemic has shown more and more companies that may be large parts of their workforce can work efficiently from remote locations.

If you are reading this book, you have an example of this in your hand. The cover and artwork for the cover of this book come from thousands of miles away from me. I e-mail the instructions, and my cover comes back in two days or less as an e-mail attachment, all paid by credit card. The cover maker does quality work; the only thing that I am interested in. I really don't care if it was prepared in an office or a basement or a bedroom.

If it is possible for highly skilled people to work from any location, then it becomes far easier to live in a place you really like where it's possible to own a home of your own instead of maybe paying $3,000 or $4,000 a month for an apartment in a crime-ridden high-cost city with no chance to ever really get ahead.

Chapter 11 – Fiscal Restraint

There is almost no one in politics or the Federal Reserve, which is also politics, that talks about a balanced budget anymore. In the old days of only a few years ago, they would have dog-and-pony shows now and then about balancing the budget, always in the out years when they would be safely retired. Now they have more or less given up on even that scam.

As of this writing, we have passed a three trillion-dollar spending bill in response to the pandemic, and the President and Congress are fighting over the second bill of one and a half to three and a half-trillion dollars – all money we don't have; not one penny of it. No one in the country knows where all of this will lead. Let's say that again -NO ONE. But we only have a few possibilities; none of them good. We could have, at some point, hyperinflation. Think of Germany after World War I; wheel barrows filled with worthless currency to buy a loaf of bread. We in this country have never had hyper-inflation. We got a good way down the road to that during the Carter administration but got it reined back in, or we could have deflation with almost all assets losing value. Debtors like inflation - you can pay off debt with cheaper dollars. Savers or people with safe money may do well in deflationary times. Or the third choice might just be a repudiation of our debt. Just admit we can't pay. A common name for that is bankruptcy.

My basic point is no one knows the outcome of all of this. A trillion dollars is an almost unimaginable number. We have President Trump promising, if re-elected, to do away with the Social Security tax on individuals, and just pay it out of the general fund. We really don't have a general fund. It's just a word. If it actually comes to pass, maybe forty-eight to fifty percent of the population of workers would be completely untethered from any tax liability for wages or social security. They could vote with impunity for any taxing scheme in the world with no financial effect on them at all; not at all what we need.

Having the pandemic in the last part of an election year is like having a major crisis and a political bidding war at the same time.

Chapter 12 – Deferred Maintenance

Go to almost any town or city in America, find a nice middle of the road neighborhood, get out of your car and walk for a few blocks, and look closely at the houses. You will see a lot of work that needs to be done; roofs that need replacing, driveways that are crumbling, and a lot of painting and siding work. Most of this deferred maintenance is not because the homeowner doesn't care. It has to do with ever-rising real estate taxes. In a lot of cities, you pay for your house again every fifteen to twenty years in taxes. So the house you bought with a thirty-year mortgage and paid off with a lot of hard work, you've actually paid for three to four times the original loan plus interest and thirty years of real estate taxes that never stops or slows down ever. Now maybe you're retired and on a fixed income and your savings, if you have any, generating almost no interest. So to stay in your home, you have to let things you would like to do to maintain your home slide year after year. This not only destroys families, but it also destroys the whole neighborhood.

Deferred Maintenance

Now get back in your car and drive downtown and walk the streets some more. Look at the crumbling business district and the taxpayer-funded public buildings. Many towns had a functioning court-house and jail with the first one built years ago lasting eighty to a hundred years. The new ones seem to last about thirty years and then need to be rebuilt yet again. If you could see below the sidewalks and streets, there is a lot there that needs rebuilding. You would see water and sewer lines that are a hundred years old and failing by the day. Lead pipes that actually put people's drinking water at risk. No mayor wants to be known as the water and sewer mayor or the maintenance mayor. They all want to build monuments to their time in office, entertainment venues, or streetscapes with bricks and gas lights for about four blocks in the crumbling downtown.

A large percentage of the city's money now goes to pension payments and large salaries. In a lot of cases, crime has gone up to the point where people start to leave town. There is a lot of blame to go around. Some of it is the taxpayers that keep electing the same people year after year. Cities are now budgeting big money to tear down homes that are abandoned through the inability to pay the taxes or upkeep or the ever-increasing crime rate or all of the above. It's really hard to kill a city, but a lot of our elected officials have done a good job on that if nothing else.

Chapter 13 – The Spoils System

The political spoils system works just like all organized crime, and it's, for the most part, safer than organized crime. You attach yourself to an organization and a leader that is much more powerful than you are, and for a living, you do their bidding no matter what it is. But there is always a chance you might end up in someone's trunk headed for a shallow grave.

In politics, it works exactly the same way, but the chances of the trunk treatment become less, but all the rest stay the same. A young man or woman, mostly men in the old days, would go to a ward politician in a big city and ask for help to get a job. The standard question was always 'If we help you, will you help us?' If the job seeker answers in the affirmative, you would get on the city payroll with an entry-level job of some kind. Then you might be required to kick back part of your pay. In any case, your real job is working for the party, raising money, selling raffle tickets, getting out the vote, anything you are told to do. If you showed a talent for this kind of work like any job, you start to move up in the organization. You get a better city job, more pay and power, and maybe a better chance to steal more from the taxpayers. These jobs turn into lifetime employment. If your party is voted out of power from time to time, there are other institutions set up to protect you and your income and tide you over till the party gets back in power.

In the times we are in now, on the national level, you can go to a liberal or conservative think tank for a good salary, or you might end up as a paid guest on one of the news networks. Maybe you can write a book or have a book written for you. It doesn't matter what the book is about – a cookbook or a dog training book, a children's book, or a political book. The book mafia on one of the networks will see that you get a lot of airtime and a lot of sales. A good portion of the bestselling books is handled that way. In one way or another, the powers to be will reward your loyalty until the party gets back in control in two, four, or eight years. The only deal is you always, no matter what, support the party line. If you don't, the shallow political grave is waiting for you. Your whole career is one way, or another is pretty much financed by the taxpayers directly or indirectly. These are not small jobs. They're the kind of jobs that put people in three million dollar houses and hundred thousand dollar cars and kids in Ivy League schools and a lot of thousand dollar dinners and girlfriends or boyfriends on the side.

If you can keep the little people properly entertained and docile and uninformed, you can keep it going forever.

Chapter 14 – Entertainment

Think back to a time when the only entertainment was a book that, at the time, was probably in short supply or too expensive to buy or maybe a traveling circus or fair of some kind that might come to your town every few years. Most entertainments were people having a party or a dance or a church dinner interacting with other people. That was in my grandparent's time who were born in the 1880s and 1890s. My parents were born into the same world with the addition of radio and movies in the 1920s. I was born into the same thing in 1944. It was early to mid-1950s before television came to the masses. That was a tremendous change in how people managed their time. TV became very addictive from the start.

Now we have added the internet, video games, hand-held devices of all kinds and social-media. The smartphone has probably become even a more addictive device than television ever was. People can't put it down to eat dinner or have a conversation, and they tell me some people try to sleep at night with their phones on.

It's possible today to completely live in a constant world of entertainment 24 x 7 without physically interacting with another human. A lot of people seem to need continuous stimulation all day long. The worst possible punishment you could inflict on them would be to make them sit down in a quiet room for an hour without their phones or video games.

One place we are all equal is we all have twenty-four hours in our day. I don't know, and no one else does either what all this new entertainment will lead to in people's personalities over the long haul. Still, I don't think a young person can be very well rounded if they don't interact with a wide variety of people in their formative years. In the old days, kids played games in the neighborhood and made up their own rules and entertainment. It is what built a child's personality.

You'll notice I haven't talked about traditional movies. I might be wrong, but I think it's a dying industry with the movies themselves and the influence of Hollywood. The average re-run of a Law and Order hour show is better written than almost all the movies today. They cost too much to make, and it costs the public too much to see them. The days of the big movie stars are about over, and the future is probably in mini-series on television.

This new mass entertainment is also a great help to leaders and politicians. They hope you just keep entertaining yourself and they'll run the country and make all the hard decisions for you. Don't worry. We've got it all covered.

Chapter 15 – Education

We, as a country, spend a breathtaking amount of money on education. Look at a real estate tax bill from any area in the country, and the most expensive item by far is for schools. First off, it's not fair to try to put all of educating our kids on the teachers. It takes the proper backup from home to have a really good outcome. A child who comes to their first day of school that hasn't been taught anything would be a great challenge for the best teacher in the world, and there are millions of kids entering school each year like this.

My biggest hot button issue with K-12 schools is you must teach kids to read at the exclusion of all else. If you can't read and read well, you will probably be crippled your whole life. Ideally, you would start a child on their reading journey at about eighteen months and no later than two years. Teaching a child to read is not rocket science. It's just investing a lot of time in your child. You set them down in your lap with a golden book and start to look at the pictures teaching the child a basic vocabulary. See the house. See the dog. See the grass, etc. Pretty soon, you start to read the simple little words that go along with the pictures, and you are off to the races. A new reader appears before your eyes.

If I were in charge of a school district, almost all of my assets and time would go into teaching kids to read for as long as it takes to get the job done. Knowing your place in the world and knowing the history of your country and where you came from is most easily understood if you are a reader. It's all there in a good library.

When our children were born, our TV was broken. It stayed that way for about ten years. That's how much my wife and I wanted to raise our children to be readers. It was one of our best decisions ever. Maybe the best thing ever to do for your new child is to throw the damn TV into the street.

One of the biggest problems in our K-12 schools is we have a generation of teachers that weren't taught much when they went to college, and they're passing on the favor to your children. And like our politics, there is a lot of fear in teaching. Teach the party line of the teacher's union or suffer the consequences. Telling a young child that they probably won't live to adulthood because of global warming or because of systemic racism, there is no way for them to get a fair deal in life. It's the same as telling a two-year-old that there are monsters under their bed. It's a horrible thing to do and may cripple that child for life, sleeping forever with the nightlight turned on.

Education

Giving advice and consul to anyone is an awesome responsibility. As your children go through school, take the time to read their textbooks. If you find them full of propaganda instead of facts, go to your school board and make them try to justify it. The only lasting asset you or anyone has is your kids. They need to be protected from outright lies. Our professors in higher education are all competent. They know precisely what they are doing at all times. They are building a political party and a grievance society that will wreck the country in the end. And these all-knowing professors will still not be happy with the outcome they so desperately think they want.

Remember, these are the ones that a few years ago taught the teachers that are teaching your little ones now. Like most sub-standard things in government, the heavy lifting is left up to you.

Chapter 16 – The Unhappiness of the Left

It's hard for me to have liberal friends. They are always unhappy. If you go out together, the food is always tainted, or there is a bad smell coming from somehow. The portions are not evenly divided. There must be a conspiracy aimed only at them or some other slight. You have only to turn on MSNBC in the morning and catch the first five minutes of 'Morning Joe.' Mika and Joe and all the helpers and guests for the morning look like overnight Grandma and the dog both died and the house burned down. There's never a smile – only darkness and a new Trump atrocity to report every morning without fail. It looks like a stage play of the actors in 'Long Day's Journey Into Night.'

It's the same in prime time. Rachel Maddow and Lawrence O'Donnell seemed to be very unhappy people. Maybe they laugh on payday. In their shows and probably in their lives, there are only villains and heroes and no one in-between. If Hilary had been elected, we would have paradise on earth - with Trump only ruination. I have hardly ever in the last twenty years watched CNN, but their shows are the same – always villains, and nothing in life is fair.

Contrast that with FOX News that beats all the rest in the ratings most of the time. At least their people look like they might be capable of laughing and having a good time, and most of them seem to have a good sense of humor. Humor is an awfully important trait, especially in the times we are living in. A lot of things that can't be changed in the end can only be laughed at.

In the liberal mind, there is always another person to be corrected or controlled or made to see the light. Just like in a totalitarian state, there is always a new enemy to be dealt with. The hole in their souls can never be filled. These are dangerous people to put in charge of your life. Every day now, in our country, it gets harder to point this out. People get scared of losing their jobs and livelihoods and start to self-censor themselves, and freedom of speech starts to die.

You only have to look at history. It can happen in any country, even ours.

Chapter 17 – Defunding the Police

If we were in what passes for normal times these days, a lot of mayors and city council members that are advocating for defunding the police would in an election year be making a case for more funding. Any so-called leader of a city or state that would propose doing away with their police force or defunding it to a level that accomplishes the same goal has forfeited their right to lead anything, and they need mental help of some kind. We could make an endless list of why this is an insane idea, but we only have to think of a few scenarios.

Let's say it's the middle of January up in Minneapolis, Minnesota, on Route 90 that runs through the city. In the middle of a 12-inch snowfall, a semi-truck jackknifes on the highway, and there is an eighty car pileup. Police work just turned into traffic control; exits need to be blocked off; traffic rerouted; wreckers and emergency vehicles need to get to the scene, and we need to get people off the road before they freeze to death.

Or let's try this one. Your eighty-five-year-old mother that lives alone in Seattle, Washington, and you talk to from your home in Wisconsin every two or three days, suddenly isn't answering her phone. You call the Seattle PD and ask them to make a wellness check to see if Mom is alright, which they are more than happy to do if they have any manpower left.

Or there is a major structure file in Portland, Oregon, that might involve hazardous materials and a thirty square block area needs to be evacuated, police going door to door to help older people get to safety regardless of their skin color or economic status.

Or it's three in the morning, and your neighbor down the block still has his party going that started at eight o'clock with loud music, and you need to get some sleep before you go to work.

Or it's the middle of the night, and you are a young woman home alone sleeping in your bed, and your dog that hardly ever barks starts to bark and growl, and the fur on the back of his neck starts to stand up. Maybe you would very much like the police to come by and check your house.

All of these scenarios are policing, but they are also quality of life issues. Then there is the kind of situation that is hard to even think about. Your ten-year-old daughter went three houses away to visit her girlfriend and disappears -the ultimate nightmare. You need all the help in the world, and you need it now – not in an hour or two – but right now. It's your child we are talking about.

We hire the police to do a job we aren't equipped to do in our daily lives. The police see a lot of the worst that humanity has to offer - women beat bloody by their husbands or boyfriends, little children in dirty diapers that haven't been fed in two days, and the vast majority of the cops do this tough job with compassion and dedication. In the end, they have the same problems as all of us. They fear for their children and their families and the future. Are there cops that shouldn't be on the force? Absolutely! Should we hold them to a high standard? Absolutely! But we have to have them, or our civil society will break down very fast. If that happens, it may be very hard to put it back together. Our freedom and quality of life, even in the smallest things, hang in the balance.

Chapter 18 – Trump/Russia Investigation

Some of the most popular books and movies are stories about conspiracies, large and small. In real life, it would be hard to count the books that have been written about the Kennedy assassination that claimed that it was all a conspiracy or fictional stories where the evil corporate head of the company is planning to take over the world. The American people love conspiracies. Now for the last three years plus, we've had maybe the grand-daddy of them all - an actual conspiracy from the highest levels of our government to overthrow a duly elected President of the United States. If the conspiracy is true and it looks like it is more every day, it's one of the most important events in our history for a lot of reasons. The biggest thing is they almost pulled it off. Years of elected members of Congress coming on national TV and claiming 'we have the evidence locked away in a secret room in the Capital and in the fullness of time all of you will see it. President Trump is an agent of Russia, and he has clearly committed treason. We have the evidence.' And most all the press in the country was supporting the liberal liars in Congress, both print and cable.

Only a very few people in the country were really looking at what may have happened. Kimberley Strassel wrote a lot of very informative columns in the Wall Street Journal that were some of the best information available, fine expert work on her part. Mark Levin has done a lot of good work on his show on Fox News, a show that ought to be a model for a lot of shows on all the networks. One guest for an hour, a lot of really good questions with adequate time for the guest to answer, and a lot of good information.

Now to some of the people that did a lousy job on this very important story and I take no pleasure in saying this. Sean Hannity and Laura Ingram had access to all the excellent investigative reporters that, in some cases, were working night and day on this story. Every night on their shows, they would both tell you how important the story was. Then give their guests practically no time to report what they had learned and continuously being talked over and interrupted. I don't know if this is from all their years on talk radio, but neither Sean nor Laura know how to interview anyone worth a damn. They're too in love with their own voices. Sometimes you wonder why they have guests at all, and they are always pressed for time trying to keep too many of their friends employed. I think both of these people are very decent human beings, but they both let us down, maybe on one of the biggest stories in our history.

As I am writing this, the John Durham investigation is proceeding, and we may get to the bottom of things at some point. If it proves to be true that this was actually a conspiracy to unseat a President, the people involved are the people that have committed treason. They should be punished accordingly, and the people and news agencies that either didn't report on the story at all or pushed the false narrative should pay some kind of a societal price.

Chapter 19 – Climate Change

Climate change or global warming or whatever we're calling it this week was made in heaven for the left. It is, in some ways, the perfect scam. Nothing but pain and suffering and expenses now, and any possible gain will be after you and your children, and maybe your grandchildren are dead. It's inventing a new religion with a lot of payoffs for the right people—all based on the idea that the world will warm maybe two degrees in the next hundred years. But no one knows anything really for sure.

Let's have a little fun for a minute. Let's say you are a liberal college professor teaching at the University of Wisconsin in Madison and are about to take your very large pension and move to Miami, Florida. In Madison, you're living in a world where the average high temperature is 56 degrees, and you're about to retire to a world where the average high temperature is 81 degrees – a 25-degree difference. You may be killed by something in Miami, but it won't be the change in temperature.

If the global warming crowd has their way, they will mandate solar panels for every roof in the country with a payoff to you in twenty or twenty-five years, but the system on your roof won't last that long. They'll make you buy a $40,000 electric car and tell you how much water you can use in a day controlled by a smart meter. And they'll have an approved list of what foods you may eat and how much. They will ban all fossil fuels and destroy large parts of the economy. But their political supporters and corporations they prefer will, as always, do really well, and with this liberal dream, there will always be something else to ban or regulate. They're working night and day to sell this new religion to as many people as possible, especially young people.

This is the madness of the left on full display. You only have to look. If you're on the right side of their plans, you get rewarded with grant money and profits. If not, you're called a climate denier and get punished in any way they see fit.

Chapter 20 – The Surveillance State

People that have lived in the last 200 years have seen more changes than all the rest of recorded history. Someone born in 1818 could not have conceived of trains and telegraphs spanning the whole of America, let alone the advent of cars, planes or telephones. The steady advance of technology and all the sciences have given us the modern world in which we live. In untold ways, they have enriched our lives. Now the technology has advanced to a point where we have the ability to track and observe the movements of all our citizens in real-time.

I have a quiet place in the woods consisting of a few acres on a little lake in the middle of nowhere. It's a place that is quiet and populated mostly with deer and bears and all manner of small animals and birds. It's been a place of quiet and renewal for my family for over 40 years. If you were to put in the coordinates of my property into Google Earth, you would see me standing near my little house, burning a small pile of brush with a column of smoke rising into the air. So now, the whole world can see into my private place of renewal and sanctuary.

I think this is a harbinger of a world that, in the end, may take away all our quiet places and maybe our liberty. Only time will tell.

With facial recognition software and GPSs in almost everything and with quickly going to a cashless society, you can pretty much believe that you're being tracked or observed a lot of the time. It's no way to live in what is supposed to be a free country. 9/11 brought a lot of this on. It turned all the gray men loose to monitor you day and night.

Chapter 21 – Public Works

I had always wanted to build a 26 by 36-foot garage on a piece of property that I own. Basically, it's a box with an 8-foot overhead door and a walk-in door; wood construction, 16-inch on center 2 x 4 walls, and 2-foot on center trusses for the roof and quite expensive wood siding and a concrete floor with frost footings. Two or three times, I had the money almost saved to do the job and had to use it for something else more pressing. Finally, the time arrived when I could start to build. I wrote out a material list and specifications on a single sheet of paper with a simple contract and hired a contractor to do the complete job. The only work I did was staining the siding. When my new garage was done and wired for electricity, the total cost was $19,200, 936 square feet of a garage at the cost of a little less than $21 a square foot.

Almost two years to the week after I built my garage, I was at a small nine-hole golf course that's run by a city in my area. They had just completed a new maintenance garage in which to store equipment. It was almost identical to my building. The only difference, it was 26 by 40 foot, 1,040 square feet, 140 square feet larger than mine.

Their total cost was $82,000 or $79 a square foot, $58 more than my building. Their building had started with a $7,000 architectural drawing for a 26 x 40 box. The drawing was completely unnecessary. This is just a very small example of how governments on all levels literally throw money away.

There are so many examples of tremendous waste you could list them forever. Look on the internet for the story of the Boston Big Dig in Boston, Massachusetts, estimated to cost at the beginning three billion dollars and ended up at over fifteen billion. Most of the work was substandard, and repairs started from day one. Or the California Bullet Train, tens of billions of dollars spent on really nothing and now classed as a boondoggle but still has people that are big boosters and believe it ought to go on. President Trump is pushing for a new FBI building on the same site as the old one for one and three-quarters billion dollars. You can bet that if this plan comes to pass, the price will creep up to four or five billion in the end. You only have to look at President Obama's shovel ready trillion-dollar scheme to see how fast you can burn through a trillion dollars that was literally burned in the street with not much to show for it.

You have politicians of both parties making speeches every day on the infrastructure needs of the country. And they're right. We have taken our maintenance money at all levels of government and put it into social welfare schemes of dubious value for a long time. With the way we go about public works in our country, there is not enough money in the world to rebuild our nation.

Chapter 22 – Immigration

If defunding the police should be dismissed out of hand by any sane person, the immigration believers of the left ought to suffer the same fate. The idea of completely open borders is insanity personified. The really hard thing to fathom is some of the most reliable Democratic voters in the country would be hurt the most by this scheme. People that live in our crumbling crime-infested cities with very high poverty rates that need all the jobs we can produce will be the people hurt the most. Dreams and forward progress are built on steady jobs, along with a feeling of self-worth. We will always need immigrants to come into our country, but it has to be some kind of orderly process. But the first jobs we produce should always go to the people that are already here. Some whose ancestors came here on slave ships should have the first chance to better themselves.

There is a lot of talk of reparations for slavery. The best reparations you could have would be such a vibrant economy that everyone now in the country could prosper. We have wonderful landmass in our country, still a lot of open spaces and opportunities everywhere. We're energy independent and can feed ourselves many times over. However, we spend our days fighting over mostly insane things instead of trying to improve the quality of life for all our people.

Chapter 23 – Bureaucracies

It should be a law of nature that all bureaucracies and most institutions at some time break down, both government and private. In almost all cases, they are run by people drawing very high salaries, but that doesn't seem to be enough. They start to live entirely on their expense accounts and other perks. In addition to their very high pay, they may begin stealing from donated funds. As of this writing, the National Rifle Association, a protector of our second amendment rights, has a scandal in their organization. And the United Auto Workers also has a scandal going on right now, stealing member's money so they can live like billionaires. Charities of all kinds become personal piggybanks for the people in charge. Bill and Hilary Clinton have done quite well with their charitable organization. Thirty-plus years ago, Senator Dole's wife Elizabeth had a salary of over $500,000 a year running the Red Cross. There was no scandal there, but it seems like a very high salary for an organization that always asks a lot of ordinary people for donations.

All of this should make people mad, but they seem to keep giving these institutions money.

Bureaucracies

So maybe, in the long run, no one cares. It should be at least demoralizing to most people

Chapter 24 – Wars Not Won

The only institution left in the country that not only has our respect but with a lot of people, including me, our love. This, of course, is our military, the people that always pay the real price with death and horrible wounds. Our military is designed to, if needed, knock the enemy flat. To completely subdue the enemy as it did in World War II - not to go to an awful neighborhood and get all shot up and then come home with no real gain. General Eisenhower was more than glad to let the Russians take Berlin house to house. It was a complete blood bath, and he was also happy to have a plan that would allow the French to take Paris, which he figured was another hand-to-hand affair before the Germans abandoned the city. Urban fighting almost always gives our enemies a much stronger hand. We never seem to learn these lessons, or maybe some people in power from time to time don't really care. Wars are and have always been a great way to make a lot of money. We send our soldiers to unwinnable places like Viet Nam or Afghanistan or all over the middle-east with really no chance for a successful outcome. And then they come home with their horrible wounds, both physical and mental, and we send them to a god-awful dirty, understaffed VA hospital and try to make them whole, or we depend on charities to help them. Think of how we treat our heroes in the richest country in the world.

At the end of President Eisenhower's term in office, he gave his speech on the military-industrial complex, a very important warning then and now about the people and industries that always profit from war. There are many leaders on both sides of the political aisle that have been warmongers for a long time. If you go to war, it's to subdue the enemy to a point where at least for a long time, they cannot engage in any more threats to us or the world at large. If you don't do that, you become a peacekeeping force where you become nothing but target practice for your enemy. They will kill you one at a time on their timeline. We haven't won a war in a long time. We gave up in Korea when we had the power to win and tied down tens of thousands of troops there since the 1950s. Someplace in America, in a dusty drawer, there may be an estimate of what we've spent there, but I have not been able to find it.

We have had a lot of presidents of both parties that have made some horrible decisions, and it has cost us in both blood and treasure but especially blood.

Chapter 25 – Some of Our Presidents

I was only one year old when Harry Truman became President. I will always be thankful that he decided to drop the bombs on Japan that ended the war. I have almost no doubt that I would not have known my father if he hadn't. If you go back to Truman's time, it seems like a different world; I guess it was.

When Truman left the office of the presidency, he and his wife got on the train and went back to Springfield, Missouri, and lived more or less like ordinary people of the time. There was no presidential pension in his day. At some point in his retirement, Congress allotted the first presidential pensions of $25,000 a year. Truman used to walk down to I think it was a Howard Johnson restaurant for lunch by himself with no secret-service.

Contrast that to our last three presidents. Bill Clinton single handily destroyed what was left of the grandeur of the White House with his behavior. Since leaving office, he and Hilary have gotten in any possible thing they could to make hundreds of millions of dollars. Then we have George W. Bush, who, along with Tony Blair, decided to be war-time presidents, but they attacked the wrong enemy. Saudi Arabia attacked us, and they attacked Saddam Hussein. They destabilized the rest of the middle-east with more blood and treasure down the drain. Then we come to President Obama, our first African-American president that showed significant progress in the country in civil rights. He was in a unique position to bring the country together, but he turned out to be an angry little man with scores to settle. Unlike Truman, they have all done very well in retirement.

If you take out Covid-19, President Trump has given us a good economy and kept us out of any wars and is trying to get us out of the ones we are in now. And he may be the only President, at least in modern times, that it has cost him money to take the job. He takes no pay, and I would be surprised if, in the end, he takes a pension. It's pretty hard to buy a man like that, and as always, he asks the questions that no other President has, and there is absolutely no debate that he is the most accessible president we have ever had.

Chapter 26 – The House and Senate

If you are thinking of a long career with good pay and short hours that borders on lifetime employment, you couldn't do much better than to run for a Congressional seat from some district in a big city. When you get in office, if you take care of the home folks, you can probably stay forever even if you're indicted for some crime or they find a body in your trunk. As you move up in seniority in the House and become the head of a committee or two, you will be a very powerful person that really doesn't have to answer to anyone.

The House of Representatives is full of little prima donnas that are elected by a very few people. They can stand in the House and call other people traitors to the country or foreign allies with impunity daily and have no one to answer to for their personal shortcomings or transgressions. Most committees in the House are now set up to try to embarrass and browbeat their political enemies, not to be used for real information gathering that might be tied to future legislation. There's never a closely crafted bill to solve any problem; only 'Christmas Tree' bills with every liberal dream possible attached to them even if, in the end, it would be impossible to get them through the Senate. It's all just an ungovernable show.

If we go over and take a look at the Senate of the United States, we see pretty much the same thing; a hundred politicians that are very good at milling around the Senate floor, schmoozing with each other, and not much more. A few days of so-called work and then recess and off to visit the home folks. If you should be unlucky enough to be voted out of office, there is always a corporation where you will be well received or a major law firm that, at one time, your job was to regulate. Or if you are fortunate, you can get a gig selling reverse mortgages or extended car warranties. It's a wonderful life if you are on the inside.

Between these people and lifetime appointed Federal judges that can tie-up the whole country for months or years with some insane ruling, you can see why we're at a point of being almost ungovernable.

Section 2 – Making Yourself Stronger

The people that make the rules control the game - don't let them control you. There are very few rules that, as a good citizen, you need to obey – a very few. You need to be honest in your dealings and not hurt or injure your fellow citizens. Other than that, in what still passes for a free country, you can make up your own rules for how you want to live your own life. This is a radical and dangerous concept to the left in our country. They want to control everything.

I have, for most of my life, refused to play by other people's rules, which is, in some ways, a hard way to go. Nothing in this section is a 'you must do.' Only some things I have done to make myself stronger and more prosperous or the most important thing of all, to be happy in your life. Telling someone how to live their life is an arrogant act, and giving advice is an awesome responsibility. The best advice is things you just may never have contemplated from people that aren't trying to sell you anything. In the end, only you know what is right for you, the best way to lead your life with happiness and dignity.

So there isn't any confusion in the chapters where I talk about money, which is a lot of them. I'm talking mid-west prices, not the coasts where in all cases, the prices will be a lot higher. One of the greatest luxuries you can have is to be in a position to be able to say no, I'm not playing by your rules. I have made myself too strong for you. I am a free agent. You can't dictate to me anymore. I am free.

Chapter 27 – Humphrey Bogart

Humphrey Bogart, one of the most famous actors of all time born in 1899, started his movie career in 1928 and went on to star in over seventy movies till he passed away in 1957. In the time Bogart started acting, all the movie companies had what is known as the 'studio system.' You worked for the movie company under contract. You were known as a contract player. The company told you what movies you would be in and with what co-stars. You had no choice in the matter. Also, what image you would present to the public or what people you could date or be seen with in public. In other words, they more or less ran your life. You got work and the company controlled everything.

The vast majority of the rising stars that worked under that system locked themselves into a lifestyle of movie stars—the most expensive homes they could afford, fancy cars, and out on the town most nights. Bogart had a hard and fast rule in his life. He always lived at least thirty percent under his income level. He lived like a man with a good job, not a movie star. He had a comfortable home in a good area of the city but far from a mansion. He drove himself to work in an average car with no entourage or group of hanger-on's to support.

After being dictated to for about ten years in the studio system, he was in a financial position to refuse parts for movies he didn't want to play. Twice, the powers-to-be threatened to fire him. Both times he called their bluff. He had become strong enough to change the rules of the game in his favor.

I was told this story many, many years ago by a very successful man that knew Bogart well. It's a very powerful concept to pay yourself first, make yourself strong and secure, and then you can start to write the rules of the game. There is an old economic rule that applies to most people. Your standard of living almost always rises to meet your income, and that's the great trap that keeps you playing by other people's rules. You could do a lot worse on a rainy Saturday afternoon than to watch a couple of Bogart's movies like the 'Maltese Falcon' of 'Casablanca.' Not only are they great movies, but they depict a much simpler time, maybe a better time in America.

Chapter 28 – Lucky Girl

I went all through junior high and high school with a very lovely girl. We were friends from the start. We were never boyfriend and girlfriend, just good friends, and in a way, that made our friendship even more special. She lived a middle-class lifestyle, nothing out of the ordinary, no hint of great wealth in the family. She never had a car in high school or anything that most of the other kids didn't have.

In 1965 when she turned twenty-one, she was given a trust fund by her grandmother of one million dollars. The money was in tax-free municipal bones paying five percent interest per year. My friend was still living at home with her folks, and she worked fulltime in a dentist's office. With her first year's tax-free income of $50,000, she purchased a new all brick home of about 1600 square feet in a nice sub-division for $35,000 cash. And a new Oldsmobile convertible for about $2800, and started to furnish her new home a piece at a time with used furniture she refinished herself in her garage. And she kept her job. In those times, there wasn't a lot more to buy; no cable television bill, no computer, and no smartphone with a big monthly bill. In 1965 with a $50,000 tax-free income and a million dollars backing you up, it would have been easy for her to have gone hog wild. But at twenty-one years old, she had already established her rules for living her life, awfully good rules and an awfully good person that I was very lucky to know. She passed away too young, a lot of the really good ones seem to.

Chapter 29 – A Good Decision

My wife and I got married in 1968. By 1976 we were in a position to build our forever home to live in and raise our two children. We had a choice of two different counties in which to build our house, the one we were the most familiar with, and it would have been our first choice. But after a hundred years of very conservative governance, it was starting to be taken over by the liberals, which were starting to loot their citizens every way possible. After a lot of research on our part, we chose to build in the second county, which was much more conservative and only three miles away.

Those three miles have made a tremendous difference in our finances. As close as I can calculate, in the forty-four years, we have lived in our home, we have, by our decision to build where we did, saved about $112,000 in real estate taxes. That's huge money for us, and as another bonus, we ended up with a better school system, less traffic and crime, and a better quality of life.

You can make a few decisions in your life that, in the end, will pay big dividends. The vast majority of people will only take in so much money in their life, and all too soon, you get old and may have to slow down or quit working altogether.

Try to write the rules for your life, so you end up with as much of your lifetime earnings as possible. Some places in the country treat you much better than other places. Try to find a place that doesn't rob you on a daily basis.

Chapter 30 – Food

Everyone needs to eat every day. One of the best and most important skills you can have is to know how to cook your food and have a kitchen to do it in. A lot of people are in love with their kitchens, granite countertops, six-burner stoves, triple ovens, and refrigerators that cost half the price of a new car. People spend more money on the kitchens than the average house used to cost. If you can afford it and it's important to you, go for it. But it's really not necessary to make wonderful meals.

If you drive around the city near me, every night of the week, you wonder if anyone is home cooking a meal. The restaurants always seem to be full. One of the biggest things we do in the country for entertainment seems to be going out to eat, breakfast, lunch, or dinner. There's a restaurant not far from our home that's only open for breakfast and lunch. It's a pleasant place with very good service and adequate food. If my wife and I go there for breakfast, usually eggs, bacon or sausage, toast, and coffee with a twenty percent tip, costs about $32. You see mostly older people. With a family of four with two hungry kids and a twenty percent tip, you are talking at least about $70. That, to me, is too much. I'm not saying the restaurant is overcharging. The restaurant business, in the best of times, is a hard business to make money in. All I am saying, it's too much compared to eating the same breakfast at home. For two people for an actual cost of $2.15, I'm figuring the hassle to make it is canceled out by the hassle of driving to the restaurant, and that's not even figuring gas.

Now, if you start talking about dinner, in our area, we have every steakhouse chain in the world. Two dinners at one of them, a 16-oz ribeye, baked potato and a salad with no appetizers, will run you at least $80 to a $100 with tip but not including drinks. The same meal at home with the best rib-eyes you can buy costs less than $32. Throw in a pound of cooked shrimp, and you are up to around $40. A couple of times a year, my wife fixes a prime rib dinner for the nine people in our extended family. With the prime rib, you might as well say all you can eat, potatoes, salad and several side dishes. She budgets about $150 for that meal, and there are always leftovers.

Not long ago, we had that same dinner out with the same nine people for a very special occasion. The restaurant was very nicely decorated, but it was extremely noisy and almost impossible to have a pleasant dinner conversation. The tables and chairs were not very comfortable and too close together, and our prime rib, potatoes, and salad were only fair, and the service was uneven. For that, we forked over a little over $600, a $450 difference from home. If you can afford to eat out all the time, more power to you.

If you're a young person with your first job and trying to pay off student loans or trying to set up your first household, you may need to learn to cook at home for a while. Between high rents and high car payments and phone and cable bills, the rules that someone else set up for you, they may keep you broke for a good part of your life. There may come a time in the not too distant future when it will become necessary to cook at home for a while. With pandemics and riots and looting, it might be a good idea to have at least a two or three weeks supply of something to eat on hand, food that doesn't necessarily have to be refrigerated. So you have the luxury of not having to go out for a while.

With all the global warming scams out there, brownouts and blackouts may become the order of the day. There is no such thing as absolute security, but the people that plan ahead generally do the best when things start to fall apart. And it doesn't cost you a dime to have a plan.

Chapter 31 – Little Things That Add Up

I am a coffee drinker. If coffee was alcoholic, I'd be a hopeless drunk. About thirty years ago, I realized I was stopping at least three times a day for a cup of coffee. So I went to the store and purchased a real large metal thermos. I would fill it religiously every morning and take it with me on my daily travels. I estimate it has saved me a small fortune. Three cups a day purchased for $2 a cup equals $6 a day, five days a week, which equals $30 times fifty weeks a year equals $1,500 times thirty years equals $45,000. Not too bad a return for buying a thermos. If I had been a soft drink man, I would have purchased a small cooler and done the same thing. When I started to do the thermos bit, coffee was less than $2 a cup, but in the end, it was about $2.75 to $3.

At one time in the country, you never saw people carrying around bottles of water as they do now. The only people in the old days carrying water were in the desert or doing hard physical labor. Now a lot of people, my wife included, so I am trying to be careful here, take a bottle of water almost everywhere. I understand the concept of being hydrated, but it seems like overkill to me. There is absolutely no future in buying water unless your water at home is undrinkable. Get a thermos and start to save a lot of money. Buying a bottle of water at a convenience store for $2 or a soft drink for a $1.50 or a latte for $7 or $8 is designed to keep you broke. A family of four or five could spend a fortune on drinks on vacation, just stopping a couple of times a day for gas.

Buy a couple of thermoses and a cooler, and you can rewrite the rule for a fortune in spending over your lifetime. It is a minimal investment that will pay better than anything in the stock market with no downside potential. An awfully lot of people have no clue at the end of the year where all their money went. Don't be one of them. It's your money, no one else's.

Chapter 32 – Transportation

There should be a lot of things for the car companies to be afraid of. First, it may be no one, or not enough people will buy into the electric plan that they have invested nearly all their money in. Second is we're up to over $34,000 in average transaction price for a new vehicle. If you're only talking trucks, it's over $40.000. They have gone to seventy-two and eighty-four-month financing, and it's still hard to get a lot of people financed. Second, there are a lot of sub-prime loans out there, with default rates going up every month. And the third thing is a lot of young males in the country don't care about cars anymore. A lot of them don't even have a driver's license. When I was in high school, every kid in the place was counting down till their sixteenth birthday so they could get their driver's license and get out on the road. In a lot of big cities, it's much cheaper with high insurance rates and high parking fees to use a car service of some kind when you need to go somewhere.

I have known a lot of people in my life that have always been car poor, a car payment their whole adult life and maybe more than one in a married family. And that was in a time when cars were about a third of the price they are now. If you take total car expenses for a lot of people, it will get close to or even exceed their housing expenses. I have only purchased one new vehicle in my life, a 1991 Chevy Extended-cab pickup truck. At the time, it cost me $19,200. I had to finance it over five years. My truck just had his 29th birthday. He has never been babied, only serviced regularly and washed. With the price of new trucks to replace mine would be close to $50,000. My truck is now going up in value. It's still worth about $8,000. The only way I could justify the $19,200 was to think about it as a long-term investment and to be free of any car payments for the last twenty-four years. I think we are starting to see a new cottage industry in the country. If my truck with its good body was mechanically worn out, I could put in a new factory engine and transmission with a factory warranty with labor and new brakes and shocks for about $12,000, less than one-third the cost of a new truck today.

For a long time, cars and trucks, like a lot of other things, were 'use them and throw them away' but now that may be changing. Things that make economic sense start to be embraced by people.

Try to find some way to beat the transportation trap. It's another place where you can rewrite the rules and end up in the end with a much larger net worth.

Chapter 33 – Housing

A long time ago now, I had a young man who worked for me. He was twenty-two years old and was about to get married. One day I just happened to ask him where he and his future wife were going to live. He told me that between the two of them, they had saved about $7,500. They planned to rent an apartment and buy all new furniture and a new car to start their life together. I went home that night, thinking about what he had told me. Two days later, I asked him if he could meet with me with his future wife after work. At our meeting, I told them I thought they were making a big mistake. In those days, you could buy a really nice home for about $30,000. I showed them that with $6,000 down, they could be in their own home for not much more than the rent they planned to pay. I told them to forget about the furniture and the car and concentrate on buying and trying to pay off the house while they were both working before they started to have children.

Long story short, they took my advice. I found a good honest realtor, and they ended up buying an all-brick home in a nice neighborhood for $28,000 with $6,000 down and a 15-year mortgage. They lived with their old car and hand-me-down furniture and paid the house off in less than six years – free and clear. They still live there to this day. The home is worth over $200,000, and it allowed the wife to stay home for a number of years to raise their two daughters. And my young friend has had to change jobs four times in his career with periods of unemployment, but it never really hurt them that bad. They had the big thing taken care of a paid-for home.

The advice I gave them all those years ago was the advice I got from a wealthy man that didn't look like he had a dime. He told me, "Kid, just buy the nicest house you can afford in the nicest neighborhood you can find and find a way to pay it off. Then put some money in the bank for taxes, and no one can hurt you ever. You can always get bread to eat."

In the area I live in, you can rent a decent apartment for about $800 a month, $9,600 a year. If you figure a comparable home would have a tax bill of at least $4,000, you are down to $5,600, and you can start to take off all your home maintenance expenses. In a case like that, you may be OK renting, but if you're paying rent of $3,000 to $4,000 a month, you better have an awfully good income, or you may never get ahead.

At one time in the country, we were mostly a one paycheck family. Then we added the second check. And then we invented the home-equity line of credit. That's really the third paycheck. That is the reason why a lot of people of retirement age have little or no equity in their homes, playing by other people rules to keep you broke and docile. You're much better off with a 1600 square foot home you can pay off than with a 4000 square foot home with a $10,000 tax bill that's never going to go away.

If you look on Friday in the Wall Street Journal real estate section every week, you can see some of the old and new rich building 40,000 square foot 'hotels' in which to live. Most of them are either trying to impress or trying to fill a hole in their souls that probably can't be filled. No matter the size of your home, you tend to live in one or two rooms most of the time.

After World War II, most of our veterans came back to a new home of no more than 1000 square feet with one bathroom, and no one died. Now it seems every kid in the house must have a full bath for themselves. No wonder so many kids are so unhappy when they finally have to leave home to be on their own and pay their bills, and reality starts to set in.

Chapter 34 – Building a Support Network

It's always the case that the more self-sufficient you can be, the better, but you can't stand alone against the world. You need a support group; your family first, then your friends and maybe your church or some other club or organization to which you belong. Work on your personal skills. Almost everyone has something they're good at that might be of help to someone else. If you're home all day, you might be the emergency backup for child care for someone for a day or two in an emergency. And the person you help might be able to fix a leaky faucet for you or even install a new water heater. You might be able to make a spreadsheet on your computer for someone in exchange for some service in the future or just to build goodwill.

Talking about mutual security between you and your neighbors or with your neighborhood watch, especially in these times, might pay big dividends. Try to build what in the old days we called the old boy's network - trading services to save money and build friendships. Your group doesn't have to be large or very structured, only friends helping when they can. It's awfully nice to have more than your eyes on your property at night. Most of us do that naturally in our neighborhoods. If a child or even a dog is lost for a few minutes, almost everyone turns out to help. If the present trouble in the cities comes out to where you live, you'll want all the support you can find.

I know it's very demoralizing and scary to even think about things like this, but it is what it is. Make all the friends you can. It's a good thing, no matter what happens.

Chapter 35 – Guns

First off, let's talk about what never gets thought about. Right this very minute, while you are reading this, in more than one hospital in the country, someone who was just shot in the chest with a bullet of 115 grains to 230 grains is being prepped for surgery. When the trauma surgeon gets the patient's chest open, he can start to see the horrible damage. What path did the bullet take? Did it bounce off a rib and go through a lung or maybe the heart? Did it stay in one piece, or in the case of most hollow-point bullets, did it splinter into fragments? Did it stay in the chest cavity or exit – may be out the patient's back or anywhere, even a leg? How will the surgeon ever start to try to repair the damage or save the patient's life?

Shooting someone or being shot is a horrible, horrible event. Probably the worst thing you can do to another human being. And in big cities and small, it's happening more and more - people standing in the street shooting at each other and killing children and other innocent people a block away.

Almost all the people on cable news and print news on both sides of the second amendment debate don't really know much about guns. You always hear that there are approximately three million guns in the country. There is really more like five or six million and more high capacity magazines than you could count in your lifetime. Gun and ammunition sales are at an all-time high. People with no experience or training with guns are buying them in droves for personal protection. If you're a new or even an old gun owner, there is a lot of things to consider when owning a gun, an awfully lot of things.

First, let's talk about the Trayvon Martin George Zimmerman case that happened in 2012. George Zimmerman, a member of a neighborhood watch in Sanford, Florida, sitting in his locked pickup truck with a handgun, saw seventeen-year-old Trayvon walking in the rain with his hoodie on through the sub-division that Zimmerman was guarding. Zimmerman called the police and reported a suspicious person. He was told to stay in his truck, and the police would handle it. But Zimmerman got out and confronted Martin. At this point, we won't ever know exactly what happened. There was a fight, and Trayvon ended up shot dead. What we do know for sure, it was a reckless act on Zimmerman's part, and he should, in my opinion, have gone to jail for a long time. He was charged with second-degree murder but found not guilty by a six-member jury. He was defended vigorously from some house-hold names on the right, which in this case anyway were not very smart.

The moral of this story is if you are a gun owner, don't ever put yourself in a jackpot like this. Let's say one night you're home safe in your house, and you hear someone breaking into your car in the driveway. Call the police, maybe yell out the window that the cops are coming, but don't take your gun and go out and confront the robber. If it turns out to be the fourteen-year-old neighbor kid and you shoot him, at very least, it might cost you your life savings and possibly your home in attorney's fees to try to stay out of jail. The only time you use the gun is if someone is physically breaking into your home, and in that case, if you shoot the intruder, you will still have to defend your actions in some way.

In my life, I have held three people at gunpoint. I would have been justified in shooting anyone of them. One later turned out to be a murderer. In two of the cases, I was able to retreat safely. Don't ever buy into the 'stand your ground' theory. If you can safely retreat without putting yourself in more jeopardy, the smart thing to do is to withdraw. I'm very thankful that I never needed to shoot or kill anyone. You don't need the dead coming to sit at the foot of your bed at night for the rest of your life.

I'm in no way telling you not to have a gun. I've had guns all my life, but you have to be real, real careful. Putting a gun in your home if you have children may be more dangerous than the threat from which you want to protect yourself. If I could have only one gun to protect my home, it would be a 12 or 20-gauge shotgun with a 20-inch barrel. You get more respect holding a shotgun than a handgun, and that might keep you from ever having to use it. Between my wife and me, we have loaded and reloaded over 400,000 shotgun shells in our lives. So I think I know a little more than most of the talking heads when it comes to the subject of guns.

Our second amendment right is every bit as important as free speech. Let's try our best to protect both of them.

Chapter 36 – Sports and Movies

Professional sports, football, basketball and baseball, should really be a poster child for where we're at in the country - hundred dollar average ticket prices for all the team sports with football being the highest, $5 soft drinks, $8 beers, and $5 hotdogs and don't forget the $25 or $30 for parking. Then there are programs and souvenirs or sports clothes. A family of four, if they are careful, could maybe get out for $600 or $700 to see a game watching a bunch of guys making tens of millions a year. In a lot of cases, more than that, and some of them on a regular basis disrespect our flag or disparage the country in their statements. We buy hundreds of millions of dollars worth of their clothing with their numbers on the back. We watch as some of them assault their wives and girlfriends and have tremendous traffic accidents in their quarter-million-dollar cars, and we support their lifestyle without question.

The same with movie stars; we try to emulate their lifestyles. They make most of their money producing movies that depict people being shot and killed in every other scene. And then they come on television and lecture us about guns. Or they have love children out-of-wedlock but lecture us on our morals. But we still go to their movies on the first day of release and stand in line and pay $20 a ticket or more to sit in a noisy theater and maybe catch head lice as we eat our tub of popcorn that costs more than a good meal. If you turn on your computer in the morning or your smartphone to get the news of the day, the first thing you will see is about what happened in their lives overnight, either that or a story on the royal family with their unimaginable wealth, but all of their personal problems. The poor dears just can't cope most of the time, and in their personal lives, they think of us not at all, or they laugh at you for supporting them.

If you like team sports, watch your kids play at school or wait for the movies to come out thirty days later and get them from your local library. Save your money for the people you love, your family.

Don't support people that really despise you and hold you in low regard. Make yourself stronger, and they less rich. Change the rules of the game.

Chapter 37 – Jobs

Most people, unless they are very lucky, will have to work thirty or forty years in their lives to live and maintain themselves and their families. No matter what it is, blue-collar or white-collar, in the end, it's a job. You show up and do the work, and someone hopefully pays you. The conventional wisdom is if you go to a four-year college and graduate, you'll be much better off financially than, say someone with less education.

But is that really true? I know a young woman that went to a very highly-rated college and graduated. In talking with her, it's hard to know what she is really qualified to do; a lot of classes but no real skills. She has been trying to get a job in the corporate world for two years now with no success. She has about $75,000 in student loans. Now at age twenty-five, she is going to borrow a lot more money to go to law school. She's a smart girl and is attractive and presents well. But as of now, she doesn't have many marketable skills. She may very well end up approaching thirty years old with no real work history, and the world is already awash with attorneys. There seems to be a lot of college graduates around that are approaching thirty with no forward progress in their work life.

I know another young person. He is the son of a neighbor that I watched growing up. He graduated from high school and went to a junior college for two years to learn to be a welder. He got hired before he finished his courses. He lived with his folks until he was about twenty-two. Now at twenty-three, he just put a good down payment on a nice little house. He also has a nice three-year-old pickup truck paid for, and as of right now, he has savings in the bank of $90,000. In five years, he has become a pretty substantial person. If he stays on this path until he is thirty, the hard part of his life will be over. He will be by a lot of standards semi-wealthy.

I have known a number of doctors that to the person has said they never made any money till they were in their middle thirties. That doesn't leave too many years to make money unless you want to work until you are in your seventies. I have no data for this, but I would bet money that the average journeyman plumber makes more than the average attorney that has graduated in the last ten years and probably has a much more secure job.

I am in no way anti-education, but just like President Eisenhower's speech all those years ago about the military-industrial complex, someone should have warned about the educational-industrial complex. We have sold the idea that young people should go deeply into debt to learn dubious skills with maybe no job at the end of the process. They have dug a deep hole for a lot of young people that will have to dig themselves out of it at some point.

Chapter 38 – Hobbies and Fun

In the first section of this book, I wrote about some of the institutions that have so badly let us down. It was pretty demoralizing to write and probably to read. And in the second section, I have written a lot about making yourself more secure financially. Now let's talk a bit about spending money to have fun in your life. If you don't have something to make you happy, you're a damn fool. Life is too short not to have as much fun as possible.

Years ago, I knew a man who was the senior vice-president of the biggest bank in our town. One day at age fifty-six, he retired and took up the sport of skeet shooting. That's a game of shooting clay targets with a shotgun around a semi-circular course with eight shooting stations. I met him for the first time because I was involved in the same sport. I asked him one day about retiring at fifty-six. He said 'in my banking career, I have had a lot of bank customers that have millions of dollars in the bank that are in their seventies or eighties and are in poor health. To a person, they all said the same thing. All I ever did was work and make money. I never had any fun, and now it's too late for me. I was a damn fool.' My friend said one day, he decided that it was not going to happen to him. He was going to have some fun. He said if I live long enough, I'll probably be pretty much broke, but it will be a good tradeoff anyway.

Find something that brings you joy and go for it. It doesn't have to be something that costs a fortune. If you went out to buy a used boat or a snowmobile or a lot of other play toys, you would hear the same story. We purchased this boat for big money and have only used it five times in three years. We paid $20,000 for it, but if you buy it today, you can have it for $10,000. Don't fall into that trap. You can drive down a lot of streets and see a lot of very expensive play toys that only live in the driveway and never move.

You might have to prioritize to have the money to pursue your passion. I sure have. But by all means, have some fun anytime you can. You probably work hard and deserve it. If you want to go fishing on the great lakes for salmon, three or four times a year, you are far better off to go to a commercial enterprise and pay the daily fee instead of thousands of dollars to own your own boat. At the end of the day you can just walk away, with no insurance or upkeep or investment.

Always run the numbers and make the best decision you can.

Chapter 39 – Unintended Consequences

At one time in America, we had neighborhood banks. In the time before credit cards, yes, I am that old, there was Sears credit cards and Montgomery credit cards but no VISA or Master Charge. They didn't really get going strong until around 1965, and what was considered a high credit line was $800. I had one of the first cards issued. Before that, if you needed a small or large loan, you physically went to the bank and talked to a loan officer.

A week after I graduated from high school, I went into my neighborhood bank at eighteen years old to apply for a loan to go in business for myself. The loan officer that I would have usually talked to was busy that morning. So I ended up in the bank President's office. His last name was Smith, and he was a wealthy and prominent man in town. I told Mr. Smith my business plan and that I had saved $600 and needed a loan for $1,400 more. After talking to him and presenting my business plan, he approved the loan on the spot. He told me if I had any trouble repaying, come to him right away, and the bank would try in any way possible to help me.

Over the next three years, I was in the bank practically every day with deposits from my business, and I had three more loans from the bank, all paid off better than agreed. At one point, I wanted to do some business with a very well-established firm that did banking at the same bank. Mr. Smith went out of his way to tell these people that I was well thought of at the bank, which helped me tremendously to get the deal done.

To be well thought of is a very good thing in business or life. In those days, the bank closed at noon on Wednesdays. A week before Christmas, one year at 11:45 A.M, I was in the bank making a deposit. It had been snowing all morning, and there was about eight inches on the ground already. Just before closing, two men in Santa Claus suits came in and robbed the bank of over $40,000. It was quite an experience, the only time I have ever been in the middle of a robbery. One time is more than enough.

There was an African-American man named Alvin that just went by Al. He had banked at my bank much longer than I had. He had a hard life. He could hardly read or write. The best thing he knew how to do was work. He was a very big man, about 6' 6". He worked in a meatpacking plant near town. Every Friday night, he would cash his paycheck at the bank and put as much money as he could in his savings account. I found out from talking to him he had a wife and three children. He had always been a renter, and his dream was to have a house of his own. The day finally arrived. He had saved enough to make a down-payment of almost 40%. When he applied for his mortgage, he told the bank the area of the city where he was going to buy. That raised some red flags with the bank. Mr. Smith, the bank president, had Al come in for a talk. First off, he told Al the bank was more than happy to give him what he needed, and he was a valued customer. But the area where he was thinking of buying was a declining neighborhood. The bank already had some corporate loans in that area that were going bad. He suggested to Al that he buy in another area two miles away, a fully integrated neighborhood that probably had a much better future. Al was thankful for the advice and said he would change his plans. As always, Mr. Smith said we'll help you in any way we can.

Three days later, Al's minister and a Civil Rights attorney came to the bank and told them they were in violation of the Federal Red Line Law that states 'it's illegal to deny a loan in a certain neighborhood. And if they didn't give Al the loan in the declining neighborhood, they would file a federal lawsuit against the bank. Not wanting to be in violation, the bank capitulated and loaned Al the money to buy in the declining neighborhood. Eight years later, all the local businesses had abandoned the area – no local shopping left at all, and crime of all kinds was a real problem. After eight years of Al paying on his house and with his 40% down, his home was virtually worthless. His one shot at a better life was destroyed by the government getting between two good men, a banker with the best intentions in the world, and a hard-working man trying to better himself.

I don't think this was an isolated case. Over the next twenty years, the Federal government all but destroyed neighborhood banking. Now it's all large and impersonal banks that don't know their customers and couldn't care less. The government should have put people like Mr. Smith in charge of banking instead of the Elizabeth Warren's of the world.

Chapter 40 – Wealth

What constitutes wealth, and what really is wealth? If you ask most people, the first thing they would say is money, but is that really what it is? I lived with my mother and father and brother and sister in fairly nice rental homes until I was almost out of high school. We always had a fairly old car. We had enough money for food and clothes but never any extra money. We children were rich in the fact that our parents spent time with us, read to us as children, and taught us to read. They demanded that we behaved and had respect for other people. They told us stories of their childhoods, and we were also blessed to have wonderful grandparents. If we wanted extra things, we had to work to get them.

For a middle-class kid, economically, I had a very good window at a young age into a different world. We had some relatives that were very, very well-to-do. By the time I was twelve years old, I had eaten probably over a hundred meals where if you wanted a glass of milk or really anything at all, you rang a little silver bell at your place setting, and one of two maids would make the long trip to the dining room and get what you required.

This family could afford to have anything they desired, anytime. Over time, the family fell apart. They didn't do anything particularly wrong, but they never had much real happiness. At the same time, my family prospered in the things that constitute real wealth, a loving family, and long-term happiness.

We are almost all guilty of being enamored with the thought of great wealth. You see the stories in the news all the time of people with not only hundreds of millions but now billions that are like a Greek tragedy. Their children are drunks or drug-addicted or committed suicide, divorces and child custody battles, and all the rest. A lot of this is probably just luck in life, but a lot of it stems from too much money sometimes at too young an age.

If you end up with a loving family and enough money to keep the wolf permanently away from the door, then you have wealth beyond compare - all the rest is just numbers in a ledger book. It has no real meaning. Happiness and fulfillment are built on other things.

There is nothing wrong with trying to build wealth, but don't let it get in the way of what really matters.

Chapter 41 – Privacy

As a nation, we talk about personal privacy a lot. If you're talking about Google Earth, giving everyone the ability to look at your house or property or someone hacking your personal financial information, it's a debate worth having. But there is a lot of angst over privacy that is a self-inflicted wound. I started to notice this about thirty years ago, and it has gotten worse. People want to tell almost absolute strangers all the most intimate details of their lives to justify their lifestyle or seek absolution in some way. In almost all cases, if you aren't impacting someone else directly, no one really cares who you love or who you're sleeping with or having sex with. Most people would be much better off just to keep their mouths shut and live their lives. People want everyone to embrace their lifestyle or way of living.

A long time ago, most people kept their private lives a lot more private. It was a pretty good way to live. A lot of people will never accept how you've chosen to live your life. Why try to bludgeon them into accepting you? In my way of thinking, it's much better to just go about your life in a quiet way than to care so much about what other people think. I have learned a lot of valuable things from people that chose to live their lives out of the accepted norm without really having to intrude on their privacy.

A large part of our politics today is a party that demands uniformity in everyone's thoughts and actions. As long as a person is honest and law-abiding, they have the right in our country to seek happiness in their own way without having to justify it to anyone else. Just keep what is private – private. And try to be happy.

Chapter 42 – Summing Up

There's always some old guy sitting in his easy chair telling you in his time things were a lot better, and now the world has gone to hell in a handbasket. I guess that I am that old man now, but I know one thing that was a lot better, and that was growing up in the time I did - from walking to school three blocks alone at five years old in kindergarten, across a busy street. To have jobs delivering newspapers, cutting lawns, shoveling snow, and at fourteen, working three hours a day cleaning up at the local gas station for one dollar an hour, cash. Making my own deals for payment and putting a lot of dollars in my blue jeans, working for wonderful people, and a few bastards. My parents were wonderful, careful people, but as long as I did good in school and behaved myself, I was a free agent, and all of my friends were more or less the same way. We were all little capitalists with our part-time jobs.

Kids today are almost completely deprived of that experience, and I think that's one of our biggest tragedies. We have a couple of generations at eighteen or twenty-two and just out of school, are completely unprepared for a world in which all of a sudden they're not special to anyone other than their parents. At eighteen in my time, most kids had worked at something and had had some disappointments and setbacks. In other words, they had some coping skills. You learn that every day might not be great. You learn just to put your head down and get through it. Tomorrow might be better. A lot of kids today expect only perfect outcomes all the time. I think the best gift you can give your children or grandchildren is to make them tough enough to go out into a tough competitive world.

I have spent a lot of time in my life observing animals. They all teach their offspring survival skills, so they have the best chance of surviving. Also, make your kids learn the real history of our country – the good and the bad, so some bogus argument can't fool them. Encourage your children to debate and argue with you on any subject. The only rule for this is that they have to have some facts to back them up. I grew up in a family where the kitchen table was debate central, but you had to argue facts, not emotions. That is not an argument. If you have a ten-year-old child that can't leave the house or the yard unless they're supervised, that means you're building a cripple maybe for life right before your eyes.

We're about at a tipping point with the number of voters in the country that know none of our country's history. Politicians get up every day and lie through their teeth, and a lot of potential voters really have no point of view or long-held beliefs. The politician that makes the last emotional speech gets their vote. Our fake news channels and cults of celebrity worship of all the wrong people are killing what's left of our civil society daily. If you read history, almost all the great countries or civilizations fell from within, not from outside forces. In times like we are in now when you seem powerless, it is the time to hold your family and friends close and try to control your own environment, at least. We may all have to become tougher and more resilient, more financially secure, and more secure in our beliefs that this is the greatest country in the history of the world.

Stop supporting people and companies and institutions that every day works against you. Change the rules of the game and try to prepare for the coming storm.

Section 3 – Into the Country: A Guide to Buying Rural Property

The start of the dream or idea to have a little place in the country could come from any source – a book or a TV show or a trip to the country on vacation or just the dream of a quiet place or sanctuary. It's a good and, in most cases, a reasonable dream. Like most any endeavors you undertake, there are things to consider; actually quite a lot of things that can make your journey a pleasure or a nightmare. I truly believe everything in this book has value that may help you in your quest to have that special place in the country. This is not a book for preppers or survivalists or back to the land movement people, although they may profit a lot from it too. It's more for people that might just want to have a quiet place to go with the thought of vacations or future retirement.

A TV show about Moving to Alaska to homestead hundreds of miles from the nearest store or hospital may make for good TV, but it's not reality for almost anyone. Even your dream weekend or vacation place might not be fun if it's a forty-mile one-way trip to the nearest grocery store. There always seems to be a hot new trend in country or rural living. In the 1970s and early 1980s, there was a 'heat with wood' movement. City people were running out to the country to buy wooded land to cut for firewood. Now we have the 'tiny house' movement and the 'building off-the-grid' movement. In the chapters to come, we will try to answer a lot of questions and tell a few stories along the way.

Chapter 43 - Land Sizes and Shapes

If I was with a group of people and I told them I owned a ranch that was 36 square miles, someone in the group might say it must take all day to drive across it – not true. A political township in our country is 36 square miles, and it is only 6 miles in all directions. So at 60 miles an hour, you could cross my imaginary ranch in 6 minutes. Thirty-six square miles is a large piece of land but not as large as it sounds to most people

<u>Land Sizes</u>
640 acres is 1 section of land or 1-mile square
320 acres is ½ section or 1-mile x ½ mile
160 acres is ¼ section or ½ mile x ½ mile
40 acres is 1320 ft x 1320 ft
20 acres is 1320 ft x 660 ft
10 acres is 660 ft x 660 ft
5 acres is 330 ft x 330 ft

A parcel of land might have all square sides or, in a lot of cases, may be irregular. A 10-acre open field may look awfully small, but 10 acres of woods may seem like a vast forest, especially if you have lived most of your life in the city. Some land you might encounter for sale might be listed as 10 acres more or less, which means it has not had a legal survey. My first ironclad rule is never, ever under any circumstances, buy a parcel of land that does not have a legal survey filed in the courthouse in the county you are in. Never! Never!

If you plan to build someday on your land, you also need a perk test for your septic field before you purchase the land. More on perk tests later in Chapter 9. Remember, if you are looking at 10 acres (660 ft x 660 ft), 20 acres only doubles in one direction (660 ft x 1320 ft) – not both directions.

Many rural people talk in terms of 40s when speaking of land. A 40 is forty acres. Someone will say I own five 40s up that way instead of saying I own 200 acres. The origins of that go back to the logging companies that counted their land in 40s years ago. When land gets sub-divided in a city or suburb, it goes down to lots. In the country, it may go from sections to ½ sections to 80s then 40s and to 20s or 10 acres or even 5s.

Someone that sub-divides a piece of land into three lakefront lots of 100 ft each may charge by what is called the front-foot like a $100 a front-foot no matter the size of the lot or land itself.

This book is only an overview to get you started to think about rural land in the right way. There will be many more examples to come. My second ironclad rule is Don't under any circumstances ever buy land that doesn't have legal access recorded in the courthouse. Verbal agreements mean nothing. Always be afraid of the term 'seasonal access only', a big red flag even if you own a 4-wheel drive vehicle or a snowmobile. A 10-acre wooded parcel for $2,500 with seasonal access might be worth zero to you. In the pages to come, I will go through some buying scenarios from start to finish – the good, the bad and the nightmares.

Chapter 44 - Buying Your Land

Let's skip ahead a minute and say after a two-year search; you found the land of your dreams. How do you pay for it? To get a conventional mortgage on un-improved land from a bank is very hard unless it is very close to a city, and then most banks will require approximately 50% down. A lot of rural land is sold on land contracts that work as a mortgage. The buyer and seller contract for a price and interest rate and the number of years. At the end of that time, if all payments are made, the seller provides the buyer with a clear deed for his purchase. This is a very good way to buy land with one more ironclad rule. Always have the payment go to a bank that holds the deed in escrow at the bank and takes a fee for the bank to handle the payment service.

Let's say you skip this step and pay the seller directly. Five years into a ten-year contract, the seller dies, and there is no one to carry on his or her affairs. You may end up with years of legal expenses and no deed or a deed with a cloud on the title. This has happened in more than a few cases. There is another advantage to a contract. The seller might five-years into a ten-year contract offer you a big discount on the balance if you settle up right away. This has happened to me.

Get a good lawyer for any land sale. It's the cheapest part of the transaction in the long run. The only other way to buy the simplest, but for most of us, the hardest is just to get out your checkbook and start writing.

Chapter 45 - How Far is Too Far

My family's place in the woods is 310 miles from our primary residence, five and a half hours driving time or about seven hours with lunch and stops. If it were only for maybe a two-week vacation or four-day weekend, it would be too far for most people or us. If you are coming up for a month or more at a time, it is very doable. Two hours up a four-lane highway and 30 miles off into the trees and lakes might be all you want to travel; 150 miles in say two and a half hours one-way. Maybe shorter or longer, only you can know how far is too far. The main goal is to be happy when you get there.

Chapter 46 - A Land Purchase Story

Bob and Jill, both employed in the city, had for several years gone to northern Wisconsin for two weeks of fishing in the summer. They towed their boat up each year, really the only time they used it all year. They stayed in a nice motel and ate all their meals out. Eating out was part of the vacation. One of the lakes they liked to fish best of all was about 400 acres with great fishing. A man owned 40 acres with 200 feet of lake-frontage. He subdivided the 40 into 30 back lots and deeded the 200 feet of lake-frontage for common use by the owners of the back lots and installed a dock.

Bob and Jill purchased a lot and had a 24 x 30-foot garage built with a 10-foot overhead door on one end for boat storage. They made the other side a front porch and bedroom and a sitting area. They had electric installed for lights and a refrigerator and heat if ever needed. The garage was all maintenance-free with aluminum siding. They have owned the place for almost 20 years now. They still have a nice home site on their 200 x 300-foot property but have never built.

Their yearly expenses last year were $580 taxes, $200 road maintenance, and $7.50 a month to keep the electric on all year – total $870 and approximately $30 actual electric charge for a total of $900. To stay in a nice motel in the area for two weeks in season runs $150 a night or $1,800 for twelve nights. Plus, their investment has gone up in value over the years, and their time up north is quieter and more restful. This is one of the cheapest and best outcomes that I know about.

Chapter 47 - Mineral and Timber Rights

Reading deeds and abstracts is a fascinating thing. In the old days, most land was conveyed to a new owner through an abstract of the property. An abstract is a written record of the property that might go back to homesteading days. When the land was purchased, a lawyer would update the abstract to the present date for the new owner. I have only purchased one 40 acre parcel that had an abstract, and then I also got a title policy. But if you ever get a chance to read an abstract, it will probably read like a history book.

A lot of rural land had the mineral rights sold to a third party, in most cases a large corporation, maybe 100 years ago for very little money at the time. This will not affect you in any way with a smaller parcel of land, probably up to even a few hundred acres. A corporation to mine anything probably would need to get to economics of scale, so you are talking about large parcels. Also, in most places today, it is politically impossible to start a mining endeavor.

Timber rights are where the owner sells off the right to harvest his trees at a future date. This is not common, but it is always possible. There again, a good lawyer is worth the expense.

Chapter 48 - Trees and More Trees

Let's say you are standing on a nice gravel road with your realtor looking at a potential land buy. Someone has subdivided a 40-acre parcel (1320 ft x 1320 ft) into four 10 acre parcels of 330 feet at the road and 1320 feet deep. The gravel road is an all-season road with winter snowplowing and electric and phone service on the road. All the land looks well-treed, and the ground is high, with no swampland.

Here is some information you need. What kind of trees do you have? Are they all one kind like pine trees, or do you have a good mix of species? Has the land been logged in say the last 30 years or so, or is it a more mature forest. Do any of the trees have value for pulpwood for paper or sawlogs for lumber? If you want to build a cabin or home, how many trees will it be necessary to remove? Say you put in a 200-foot driveway and a clearing for a home site. Will some of the trees you take out help defray the cost to clear and to build a driveway that will hold up many years? More on roads and driveways later in Chapter 14. Besides the realtor and knowledgeable neighbors, the DNR (Department of Natural Resources) or the farm bureau or county extension office may be a valuable resource for information. The DNR, if approached the right way, might even send someone out to evaluate your trees.

Chapter 49 - Lakes and Rivers

Like in Chapter 6, you are looking at a lakefront lot with 200 feet of lake frontage, 400 feet deep, or about two acres altogether. It is the first week of May and a really nice day. You have road frontage and electric at the back of the lot and the lake looks wild and beautiful. The realtor tells you it about 80 acres in size. The price of the land is well within your budget, actually almost a bargain.

In reality, it should be a bargain. The lake is only about six feet deep with a muck bottom and no inlet or outlet. The only fish in the lake are some stunted bluegills and bullheads. By July, the whole lake will have a green scum on it and be choked with lily pads. It is much more a swamp for fall duck hunting than a place to live on.

Do your own research on any lake you are interested in buying on. The first place is the DNR, the Department of Natural Resources, will know the most about any body of water in their area. The same is true of rivers. Some rivers are 100 feet wide or more and run virtually all year, and some only run in the spring or with a lot of rain upstream. At other times you may be able to walk across it on the rocks. The biggest question with rivers is always how high the water gets in flood conditions. If you ever build anything along a river, you want to be higher than even the 100-year flood. Two of the worst things in life is to be burned out or flooded out.

Chapter 50 - Tree Cutting and Removal

Companies in the tree removal business pay the highest workmen compensation insurance of almost anyone with good reason. It is damn dangerous work, even with professional employees and the right equipment.

If you buy some wooded land and need to clear some trees, you will start thinking about purchasing a chainsaw and doing the work yourself. For driveway or building site clearing, you will need professional help to cut the trees and remove the stumps and grading work. To cut a small tree or two or to clear deadfalls on the ground, you may want your own chainsaw, but you will still need some competent help to get started. If you buy a chainsaw, buy it from a local saw shop in the area you are doing the work in, and it needs to be a commercial model, not a lightweight chainsaw from the big box store at home. When your chainsaw breaks, you will want friendly, local help—one other tip. Buy four chains so you can have two at the shop to be re-sharpened and two in use. Many pros don't sharpen their own chains, so it is best to get that thought out of your mind.

A big old tree, notched and sawed by a pro, may have half the inside eaten away by carpenter ants and fall in the wrong direction and kill or maim the cutter in seconds. I have taken down hundreds of trees in my life and have had some close calls. I consider myself very lucky to have lived through it without injury. Part of being an adult is to know your limitations – sometimes a hard lesson to learn.

Chapter 51 - Septic Systems and Wells

If you are going to at some point build a cabin or house other than maybe a rough hunting camp, you will need a septic system and a well. To build a septic system, you will need a percolation or perk test performed by the building department before they will issue a permit. An inspector will come out near your building site, dig a hole about 18 inches deep, and one foot around. He will fill the hole with water and time how long it takes to drain into the ground; the faster, the better for a septic field. He may perform the test several times in different places

The best soil for a septic system is sand or sandy loam. The worst is muck or clay ground. Some land may be rejected altogether, and a building permit may be denied making the land unbuildable. A septic system consists of a concrete tank made offsite and delivered to the home site and the four-inch septic lines laid in a bed of washed stones. The size of the system is determined by the number of bedrooms you have and the size of the cabin or home. A well-built system will last for 30 years or more with any luck at all.

A drilled water well consists of a metal pipe four-inches or larger and a submersible pump inside the well casing at a certain depth, a water line running from the well to your building, and a pressure tank somewhere inside your building. A good well driller in the area where your land is in can tell you with great accuracy how deep your well needs to be to reach good abundant water. This varies wildly depending on what part of the country you are in.

Chapter 52 - Getting in Deep

In the early 80s, my friend Robert had a nice home and a wife and three kids, a good job and had everything going for him. In those years, heating oil took a huge jump in price, and there was a big movement to heat with wood. Robert got on the bandwagon like so many others. He installed a large wood stove and a second wood heater in his house. He purchased 18 acres of wooded land, 88 miles round trip from his home to have a private source of heat, and to save money. To hell with the oil companies! He bought a 10-year old Ford half-ton truck to haul his wood and a new chainsaw from a discount house out on the highway. Robert and his faithful Labrador started to go to the land every chance he got to cut down trees and load the truck. It wasn't too long, and he had to get heavier springs on the truck, and some other repairs and his new chainsaw was a home owner's model that would not stand up to the job. Over the next year, he added two more saws and bought a dozen chains, a log splitter, and a 10-foot trailer and finally a new 4-wheel drive ¾ ton pickup. The last nail in the coffin was a notice from his insurance company that because of him heating with wood, his homeowner insurance was going up $450 a year. It took Robert quite a while to recover financially. All of us normally smart people can get in too deep at times.

Chapter 53 - Taxes

About 40 years ago, my wife and I purchased a lot on Lake Michigan 100 feet on the water and about 350 feet deep to a road. At one time, I cleared out some down trees and did some cleaning up. Other than that, the lot has sat there all these years. We got a very good price when we purchased it. As of this writing, we have given the lake lot to our daughter. The taxes over the years have probably doubled the original price and a little more. City or county, you can always count on the taxman getting his share or more. Land with water frontage will almost always tax much higher than something deep in the woods.

Chapter 54 - Know Your Family

Only you know the make-up of your family and what they are interested in and enjoy. If they only like to go to resorts on vacation, then a cabin in the woods probably won't work for you. Will the kids get bored with maybe no cable TV or internet and in a year or two not want ever to come back?

It is not uncommon, not too far from where I am writing this, seeing a family come up from the city, hundreds of miles away, build a big place on Lake Michigan for hundreds of thousands of dollars, beautiful homes. You see the family for a couple of years then nothing for a couple of years, and then the For Sale signs go up. There are a lot of reasons for the sale signs – financial, a divorce, or simply a lack of interest after all that work. Only you know what will make your family happy.

Chapter 55 - Not a Bad Deal

About 30 years ago, four friends from near Chicago that liked to deer hunt came up to the Upper Peninsula of Michigan about 300 miles away and bought 80 acres of land, a quarter-mile wide and a half a mile deep off a sand road quite deep in the forest. They put in a driveway about 100 feet long and build a 20 x 34 cabin, actually like a garage with no overhead door. They put in a wood stove and some bunk beds. They built an outhouse a ways away, and they and their kids have used it as a deer hunting base and for fishing and snowmobiling ever since.

Their original investment was $28,000 complete - $7,000 per man. All they have paid over the years are taxes as they have no electricity. A couple of years ago, it was estimated that there was $24,000 of pulpwood on the property, and the hunting camp and land was worth $55,000 to $60,000. Not a bad deal at all!

Chapter 56 - Roads and Driveways

Just a few thoughts on driveways and roads made of crushed stone. To have a road that will stand up and not need constant maintenance, you need a base of large stones or rubble about 8 inches deep and small stones about 3 inches deep to dress the top and make it smooth. If you do this the right way the first time, your road will stand up for a lot of years with no more expense. In some cases, a well-drained sand road with not much traffic on it will be alright for a long time. The trick is to do it right the first time and only pay once.

Chapter 57 - Heating Your Cabin or House

The best fuel for heating a home is natural gas. It will probably not be available to you way out in the country, and that leaves you with electricity, heating oil, or propane. All have their advantages and downsides. Do estimates of costs and convenience and choose one. If you want to heat with wood for a backup, purchase a quality wood heater or stove that can heat a room or two and hot water or can be used to make a meal.

A conventional fireplace is almost worthless to heat more than a few feet in front of it, and it will eat wood at a rapid rate. Heating with wood full time is sleeping scared unless the heater is outside heating circulating hot water. For a hunting camp or something that is used sparingly, wood heat may still be your best option.

Chapter 58 - Getting More Than You Paid For

In a lot of rural areas, there are state and federal forests and other wilderness areas. We can walk out the back of our property and walk for miles on state forest land. It is there to enjoy with no taxes or expenses, and it is in an area that gets very few other people. It's almost like having your own private very large forest area. When looking for land, always look at maps and plat books of the area you are interested in for state and federal land and lakes with public access to add value to your land in a lot of ways.

Chapter 59 - Neighbors

Your experience in the wilds will depend on part on your neighbors, just like at home. The little 30-acre lake where I am, all my neighbors are all full-time residents. I'm the only out-of-state resident. In the 42 years, we have been here, we have made a lot of friends. It helps a lot to have people to look after things when you are gone. If you are way out in the woods with no one to keep an eye on things, you may be limited on how many expensive things you can keep at your cabin or home when you are not in residence. More privacy but maybe less security. It is certainly another trade-off to consider.

Chapter 60 - TV Shows and Other Bunkum

If you watch any of the shows on tiny houses, you will usually see a young woman under 30 or a young couple looking at contracting for a 150 to 250 square foot tiny house on wheels at $30,000 to $50,000 with the idea of living in it full-time. A 250 square foot house for $50,000 is $200 a square foot an astronomically high price, in my opinion. If you look closely, they never talk about septic systems or foundations or water delivery or how to keep these systems from freezing up in the winter. They never give you the full story. I can't help but think that after a time, crawling into your bed at night in a loft with no headroom will get old even for the very young. Give me $50,000 to build you a small house, and I do better, much better. I know a lot of people need housing that they can afford, but I think tiny homes will be a passing trend like heat with wood.

The same is true of the off-the-grid shows building on top of a mountain or 200 miles from anything constructing homes out of mud or old tires or bottles and junk with all your friends helping on weekends in places that would give an expert mountain climber pause. Most of these projects are doomed to failure, but that is never shown.

If you are thinking of a tiny house, go to a big box lumber yard that has a lot of large tool sheds or barns on display. Stand in all of them and imagine it is your tiny house and report back to me. You may think I am being too tough here, but there are a lot of better ways to go. See the next chapter.

Chapter 61 - Building a Small Cabin or House

There is a very good reason why most houses in the country are of conventional construction 2 x 4 or 2 x 6 walls, 16 inches on center and truss roofs 2 feet on center, and insulated walls with the electric in the wall cavity. In the long run, it makes the most sense, and if done properly, it will last well over a hundred years. A conventional home can be built on-site or in a factory and delivered to your site, probably called a factory-built home or a modular home. This is not a trailer home. It is standard construction in every way. If you were thinking about a cabin or a small house, let's say 600 to 1200 square feet, you might be able to get away with $80 a square foot.

In all cases, you need a good foundation of concrete construction to start. Foundations are always talked about the least when the TV shows are on. If it is talked about at all, it is usually crushed stone or wood piers of some kind. There are three types of foundations. Number one is a slab on the ground with small footings under it. Number two is a crawl space with four-foot walls and about four feet of clearance under the house, ideally with a full concrete floor. Number three is a full basement that we all know about. If you don't have one of these, you are starting out wrong from the first day.

You can make a 600 square-foot house work much better for you than a tiny house for about the cost of a new pickup truck at today's prices. Look at plans on-line or draw up your own. It is kind of a fun way to pass the time. Please don't get locked into the fad or fashion of the day. Think long term, and you will be way ahead.

Chapter 62 - Other Equipment

It is not at all uncommon to see a piece of construction equipment probably a yellow bull-dozer of some kind sitting on someone's land with trees growing up inside it. The story is always the same. Someone purchased an old running piece of equipment for what they thought was a good price, probably $5,000 to $10,000. The first time it broke with engine or transmission damage, they were horrified to learn the repairs were in the tens of thousands of dollars or much more. Sometimes it might be almost impossible to get the equipment out of the woods and into the shop just for starters.

If you have enough work to justify having a machine of some kind, think about a diesel tractor or skid-steer loader with a bucket and lift capacity of at least 1,500 pounds. A newer rubber-tired machine in good condition may give you years of service and not break the bank on repairs.

Chapter 63 - Ironclad Rules

1.   Never, ever buy a parcel of land without a legal and recorded survey in the county courthouse. Never!

2.   Don't under any circumstances ever buy land that doesn't have legal access recorded in the courthouse. A verbal agreement is not ever good enough.

3.   Only pay a land contract through a bank as a payment agent that is holding your future deed in escrow.

4.   Always retain a local attorney for your closing and always get a title insurance policy.

5.   If you have a wooded parcel of land with quality trees, make sure you own the timber rights. This would probably only come to play on larger parcels, but it is good to check.

6.   If you are buying lakefront property, do all the research you possibly can on the health of the

lake and recreational opportunities. On rivers, check for the 100-year flood.

7.   Cutting down trees with a chainsaw can kill or permanently maim you in the blink of an eye as fast as a bullet and maybe not as kindly.

8.   Never buy a piece of land that you want to build on without having a percolation test done.

Chapter 64 - An Ending Story

I have written a number of books, both novels and short stories, all while sitting at my desk and looking out at a 30-acre lake deep in the woods. The lake is owned by me and a handful of neighbors, all with about 10 to 12 acres of forest land. We purchased the land and had a conventional built modular home constructed on a good foundation 42 years ago, and it is as good today as when it was built. We have worked on the land all of these years, cutting old and dead trees and cleaning up deadfalls. It's been a lot of work and also a great joy. We have been blessed to have good neighbors, both humans and animals from chipmunks to bears and ducks and geese on the lake. It is also a place for our children and grandchildren. I hope for many years to come.

As of the writing of this little book, it is 2020 a really tough year with Covid-19, high unemployment and demonstrations and looting and fires in a lot of our big cities. If you have ever dreamed of a quiet place away from the noise of the world, it might be a time to start your search. If this book helps you save some time or money, it will give me great joy and would have been worth the effort. Thank-you.

Books by Steve Ashley

1932: Stories of the People and Times of the Great Depression
Copyright 2018

High Desert Hustle – Greenwich Time – Grandpa Jim
Copyright 2018

Life and Times of JC Rudik
Copyright 2018

Both Sides of the Road: A collection of Short Stories
Copyright 2020

Ernest Jones The Greatest Golf Instructor of all Time and Some of His Disciples
Copyright 2020

Into the Country: A guide to Buying Rural Property (e-book only)
Copyright 2020

The Coming Storm
Copyright 2020

Coming Soon
  Gloria: A Story of 2020

All books are available on Amazon.com as a print book and/or an e-book.

<u>The Coming Storm</u>

Unlike a natural storm that forms way out to sea, the storm we are facing is already on our shores. Our storm is man-made and has taken about 75 years to form. We are starting to see the path and possible devastation to come.

This book is about how the storm formed and ways as individual citizens, we can mitigate the damage to our loved ones and our way of life.

And a must-read section on buying a rural property if your dream is to escape the turmoil of the city.